D0594397

TOTAL RETHINK

TOTAL RETHINK

DAVID MCCOURT

WHY ENTREPRENEURS SHOULD ACT LIKE REVOLUTIONARIES

WILEY

Published by John Wiley & Sons, Inc., Hoboken, New Jersey.
Published simultaneously in Canada.

For general information on our other products and services or for technical support, please contact
our Customer Care Department within the United States at (800) 762-2974, outside the United
States at (317) 572-3993, or fax (317) 572-4002.

Wiley publishes in a variety of print and electronic formats and by print-on-demand. Some material
included with standard print versions of this book may not be included in e-books or in print-on-
demand. If this book refers to media such as a CD or DVD that is not included in the version you
purchased, you may download this material at http://booksupport.wiley.com. For more information
about Wiley products, visit www.wiley.com.

Library of Congress Cataloging-in-Publication Data:

Names: McCourt, David (Entrepreneur), author.
Title: Total rethink : why entrepreneurs should act like revolutionaries /
    David McCourt.
Description: First Edition. | Hoboken : Wiley, 2019. |
Identifiers: LCCN 2019010509 (print) | LCCN 2019011565 (ebook) | ISBN
    9781119565345 (ePub) | ISBN 9781119565369 (ePDF) | ISBN 9781119565352
    (hardback)
Subjects: LCSH: Entrepreneurship—Technological innovations. | New business
    enterprises. | Strategic planning. | BISAC: BUSINESS & ECONOMICS /
    Entrepreneurship. | BUSINESS & ECONOMICS / Strategic Planning. | BUSINESS
    & ECONOMICS / New Business Enterprises.
Classification: LCC HB615 (ebook) | LCC HB615 .M3783 2019 (print) | DDC
    658.1/1—dc23
LC record available at https://lccn.loc.gov/2019010509

Cover Design: Wiley
Image Credit: © David McCourt

Printed in the United States of America

V10010093_051019

Since the Industrial Revolution, through Jack Welch's tenure as CEO at General Electric, business has been about incremental change. But now business is about blowing up the existing model and looking at everything in a new way. It's time for a total rethink.

"You never change things by fighting the existing reality. To change something, build a new model that makes the existing model obsolete."

—*Buckminster Fuller*

"Imagination is the source of all human achievement."

—*Sir Ken Robinson*

"I'm not interested in preserving the status quo; I want to overthrow it."

—*Niccolo Machiavelli*

"The greatest discovery of all time, is that a person can change his future by merely changing his attitude."

—*Oprah Winfrey*

Contents

Foreword

"David McCourt is one of those entrepreneurs who has learned to success-fully create and to navigate public-private partnerships in order to increase investment in mobile and cable connectivity in areas where it has tradition-ally been deemed uneconomic.

"In the process he has made himself a very rich entrepreneur, but this is exactly what constructive entrepreneurship is all about – it's about provid-ing a service or product that people want, and/or introducing something new into the market that enhances the social capital of the region."

—Brian Morgan, Professor of Entrepreneurship at
Cardiff Metropolitan University

Acknowledgments

I would like to acknowledge and thank the following: Nick Covino for guiding me through Boston College High School; Father Hagarty, SJ, for teaching me the first of the five greatest lessons I ever learned: that any problem, no matter its size, can be solved if broken down into small actionable steps; Father Chris Johnson for guiding me through Georgetown University; my father, Frank, the finest man I ever had the pleasure and honor to know; my mother, Katherine, the Matriarch, Hero, and Rock of the entire McCourt clan; and the A-Team: Deborah, Dave Jr., and Alexandra, the greatest collection of kindness, love, and support God has ever put in one family.

I like to read a book with a shovel and dig for ideas (i.e. I like to read a book with a pen and make notes in the margin). As some people don't like to mess up their book, we left some blank pages for notes in the back.

1

Visualize the Future

"Logic will get you from A to B. Imagination will take you everywhere."
—*Albert Einstein*

Most of us, whether we are business people or political leaders, doctors or teachers, students or parents, live in the present and try to work toward the future one day at a time, taking tiny cautious steps, improving things incrementally. It's been a survival technique the human race has used throughout our evolution, but it may not be enough to save us from the dangers that lie ahead in the near future, and it may also mean that we, both as individuals and as a society, are going to miss the enormous opportunities that technological progress is making possible.

It is time for us to be bold, to be revolutionary, and to change the way we do things.

Other forces, some of them constructive, some of them destructive, are now moving too fast for us to keep up with if we continue with the old ways of thinking and acting. There needs to be not one revolution, but many, in both the ways that we think and the ways that we do things if we are going to be successful as individuals and if we are going to improve the lives of the majority of the people on this planet. Positive revolutions could also avert the potential conflicts which are brewing between those of us whose lives are getting better every day and those of us who are being left further and further behind by the increasing speed of progress.

It's easy to illustrate how this widening of the gap can come about. If you watch an elderly steam train making its way out of a station in India, you will see that it is heavily laden with people. They are clinging to the outsides and squatting on the roofs, as well as filling every carriage to capacity. It would seem obvious that there is a need for some improvement in the services being offered to the population. Now, India's prime minister has commissioned a Japanese company to build the country's first high-speed railway between Mumbai and Ahmedabad in the west. These trains will have top speeds of 200 miles an hour, far too fast for anyone to hope that they can travel by sitting on the roof, and are indicative of how fast India is developing.

It would obviously be a sign of progress to be able to eventually replace all that elderly rolling stock with such sleek high-speed trains. It would be far more comfortable and efficient for those who can afford to buy tickets and sit inside in air-conditioned comfort, but entirely unattainable to the crowds of poor who throng the stations in the hope of hitching a cheap or free ride. All they will be able to do is stand back and watch as the future shoots past them.

No one would deny that the creation of a high-speed train that travels at hundreds of miles an hour is a wonderful thing, but at the same time it will increase the gap between those who can afford to travel on it and those who can't, improving the lives of one and making far worse the lives of the other. In other words, this leap forward, which would be a great thing for the country's economy and productivity, would inevitably widen the gap between the haves and the have-nots, so the model for traveling across India needs to be rethought and entirely revolutionized in a way that will improve the lives of all those thousands of people clinging to the outsides of the trains, to make their experience closer to that of the people who will be able to afford to buy tickets on the bullet train. I don't have a solution for that particular problem, but it provides a vivid visual metaphor for the fact that every action inevitably has consequences, so we need to be thoughtful with every step we take, conscious of the effects improvements have on those at the bottom as well as those at the top.

Like those Japanese trains, civilization has progressed too far and is traveling too fast to be able to slow down now. If you want to be successful in any field at all, you can't rely on doing a bit better each year. Companies that increase their revenue by a few percentage points, individuals who marginally increase their earnings, inventors who make superficial improvements to their products, will not be the winners of the future. Simply being ambitious for success will not be enough either. We will all have to exercise enormous creativity and imagination in order to see and understand what is happening around us and work out new solutions to the problems that now face us, recognizing both the opportunities and the dangers ahead.

We need to dream big, but we also need to dream smart if we don't want the billions of people left behind on the platforms to rise up and attack the things they know they can never have and the people they know will always prosper at their expense.

> If you want to be a game-changer and really make a difference, then you have to visualize the future that you want to live in. You have to imagine yourself already being there and then look back so that you can picture the route by which you are going to get there.

We need to be bold and creative in everything we do. At a personal level, a cautious, conservative approach to risk and innovation may keep your career or business afloat for just long enough to support you and your family during your lifetime, but it will never change the world and it will never blast your personal achievements into any new stratospheres.

Before you can do that, however, you have to convince yourself that your dreams actually are attainable.

In 1985, while I was still in my twenties, I was invited to the White House for dinner with President Ronald Reagan, a former actor who had succeeded in confounding all expectations by becoming the most powerful man in the world. Towards the end of the meal I had to get up to answer a call of nature. There was a marine standing rigidly at attention outside the door.

"Sir," I said, "can you tell me where the men's room is?" "Down the hall," he barked, "take a left, on your right, Sir."

As I walked self-consciously away down the hall, the click of my heels echoing on the black and white marble, I heard the marine speak again, this time in a very different tone.

"Goose?"

Recognizing my nickname from high school I turned back.

"Hey Goose," he said, "It's Ned! Jimmy Rourke's brother." Jimmy Rourke had been one of my best friends at school, a great footballer who had gone on to play in the NFL for seven seasons, including the Super Bowl.

"What the fuck are you doing here?" we both said at once. "I joined the marines," he said.

"I got invited to dinner," I said.

"No one's going to believe this at home," he said.

As I stood in the men's room it occurred to me that he was right: no one was going to believe I was at a White House dinner at 26 years of age. So when I got back to the table, I slipped my neighbor's demitasse White House coffee cup, which was one of Lyndon Johnson's place settings (each president and first lady designs a new place setting for official dinners at the White House), into my pants and smuggled it out with me. When I proudly showed it to my father a few days later he was appalled that I would stoop to do such a thing.

"But Dad," I protested, "no one's going to believe that I was there."

For the same reason, I asked the president to sign my menu, which I'm guessing is not really what you are supposed to do at those sorts of events.

Things were very different on the night I was invited by Prime Minister John Major to 10 Downing Street, the prime minister's residence in London. This was many years later, when I was in my thirties and I was one of the sponsors of the Cambridge Film Festival. There was an odd selection of guests that night, including the tennis star John McEnroe and his wife of the time, film star Tatum O'Neal (the youngest person ever to win an Oscar for her role in *Paper Moon*) and the television presenter and businessman Sir David Frost, with a lady who seemed much too young to be his wife. On the way back from the men's room I passed any number of priceless, historical antiques, and there was not a marine in sight. I resisted the temptation to put anything down my pants; after all I was a respectable married businessman by then and my wife was with me.

We had just had our first baby and had left him back at the hotel with a babysitter in order to take advantage of this opportunity to have dinner with the prime minister. As charmed as I was to be a guest in Downing Street, it was clear to me that it was perhaps my wife that the prime minister found most enchanting that evening. I was fine with that, but eventually we made our escape, my wife shedding her shoes as soon as we emerged into Downing Street, and headed back to our waiting child, despite the PM increasingly insisting that we "really must" stay the night.

I recently ran into Sir John Major at the Merrion Hotel in Dublin and reminisced over a cup of tea. He was just as charming as I remembered, even though our paths had not crossed for a quarter of a century.

I appreciate that these are boastful little anecdotes and, as my father pointed out, do not reflect well on my abilities to act in an appropriately statesmanlike manner, but the point I am making is that it is perfectly reasonable for anyone to visualize themselves dining in the White House or dining at Number 10, building a multibillion dollar business empire, or winning an Emmy (for an educational series called *Reading Rainbow*), but if you want to turn those big dreams into reality then you are going to have to make a difference in the world – and you can only make a difference by changing the way things have been done in the past – by blowing up the model, by creating a revolution.

- Visualize the world that you would like to live in and the future that you want for yourself and your family.
- Then work out a route for reaching that destination.
- Work out what has to change to make your dream a reality and then construct a plan for making that change come about.

2

Start a Bottom-Up Revolution

"Let me say, at the risk of seeming ridiculous, that the true revolutionary is guided by great feelings of love."

—*Che Guevara*

Everything is changing fast, apart from how we think and behave. Technology and artificial intelligence are taking over many of the functions that we previously imagined would always be the domain of humans, from robots taking over jobs in factories to apps gaining control over our social and business relationships.

In the course of an average day we all interact with machines far more often than we interact with people, but our ways of thinking and making decisions have changed little since we lived in agricultural and industrial societies, even though the problems we now need to solve are entirely different than those faced by our ancestors. If we want to keep up with the changes, it will require a revolution in thinking as big as those that led us to start enclosing and farming the common land during the Agricultural Revolution and to building the factories and power stations of the Industrial Revolution that created the modern consumer world.

We each need to harness the energy which developments in technology have unleashed, for our own individual ends, if we are to benefit from the challenges and opportunities that now face us, rather than allowing them to swamp us.

Both the Agricultural Revolution and the Industrial Revolution brought enormous benefits to the human race, but they also created great injustices and conflicts of interest, many of which we are still wrestling with centuries later. Many would wonder why, for instance, a man who inherits a coal mine should be so much better rewarded than the miner who risks his life daily as he toils in the dark below ground. Why should land that once belonged to everyone be stripped of trees and parceled up to become the property of one farmer or one person with the wealth to invest, as happened in the Agricultural Revolution? Yet it is indisputable that both these revolutions did far more good for the collective human family than bad.

We have come to terms with these "realities" from history, but we are still troubled by their modern equivalents: why, for instance, should the guy who gets recruited to be the CEO of a major corporation be awarded a salary and bonus package worth tens of millions when the people who have worked every day for years on the shop floor actually creating the corporation's products and services earn only a fraction of that amount in their entire working lives? There is an enormous difference between an entrepreneur who creates a business from scratch and someone who is simply hired to manage it.

Political movements that have tried a myriad of different ways to face these problems have come and gone over the centuries, but globalized progress still marches forward at an ever-accelerating pace and the inequalities and dangers of societal meltdown continue to grow and multiply.

Being a revolutionary is the most exciting thing in the world, but only if the revolution results in genuine and beneficial change for the majority, creating a new way of doing things or a new way of thinking about things. There is no point in destroying the status quo unless you have something radically better with which to replace it. To do so would be merely an act of barbarity, but that is what politicians are doing all the time, taking us backward rather than forward. During democratic elections they make promises they couldn't possibly keep if they were voted into office; once in office they then tear things down simply because they were built by someone else. That model has to change if we are not going to end up tearing ourselves to pieces.

Sometimes a revolution in thinking becomes necessary in order to avert disaster, but people need to have a clear understanding of the issues and solutions and not allow themselves to fall prey to the fraudulent promises of politicians and others who are merely in search of votes and who actually have vested interests in maintaining the status quo, despite their apparently "revolutionary" rhetoric.

One of the most powerful triggers for revolution throughout history has been the gap between the rich and the poor, between the powerful and the unempowered – or at least between those who *feel* they are poor and *believe* that others have power over them. In reality we all have the power to take our fate into our own hands if we are willing to risk the consequences and if we can rally enough people together to support us, but most of the time we don't realize it, or we lack the necessary confidence or the energy to actually do it. At least that has been the situation in the past, with revolutions only breaking out sporadically and often ending in failure.

Now things are different because there is a groundswell of change and individual empowerment which is finally putting power into the hands of the masses. Everyone now has the potential to be a revolutionary. A banker can become president of France and a real estate developer can become president of the United States. Previously oppressed populations in the Arab world can arrange huge spontaneous demonstrations of dissatisfaction that topple governments, in some cases almost without bloodshed. The British government can be forced to leave the European Union and the American population can agree to be governed by a collection of elderly billionaires.

These seemingly illogical events demonstrate that there is an appetite for change, sometimes at any cost. They show that many people are dissatisfied with the status quo of their lives, but most of the answers they have come up with have not proved to be the most creative solutions to the problems which are causing that dissatisfaction, and some may even end up worsening the situations which are causing the dissatisfaction in the first place. Increased empowerment means we have just as many opportunities for making the wrong choices as we do for making the right ones.

History is littered with instances of huge populations being ruled over and repressed by small numbers of powerful people. Think of how few British colonials governed the enormous continent of India, how few masters suppressed the plantation slaves in the Southern US states and the Caribbean, and how few guards there were for the millions of death camp prisoners in the Second World War. In many cases the oppressors were able to do that because the oppressed had no way of communicating with one another and no way of coordinating any acts of rebellion, but technology is now providing the means for huge populations to talk to one another, to share ideas, and to enforce change more quickly than ever before. It is now possible for everyone to rise up and be a revolutionary, but still very few of us realize that or bother to take up the opportunities that are becoming available.

> The irony is that the people who are likely to be left behind because of the speed of change in the modern world are the ones who would probably be the best equipped to lead us into the future because they are hungrier for change and less risk averse. They have been through hardships which have toughened them up, and they have less to lose by taking big gambles.

History is so full of stories of how refugees have prospered when they arrived in new countries that they have become clichés and racial stereotypes. The Jews are most often singled out for their success in the diaspora, but also the Indians and Pakistanis who start corner shops and keep them open twenty-four hours a day or the Chinese who started laundries and restaurants around the world and went on to build up substantial businesses. My own family came to America from Ireland, escaping from poverty and lack of opportunity in an oppressed and stale economy, and prospered from the change, following the Irish stereotype by going into the construction business. In Boston in those days, most Irishmen became either construction workers or cops. Within a few generations, of course, all these ethnic and racial stereotypes disappear as new generations branch out into different businesses, creating some of the world's biggest corporations.

All these immigrants nearly always arrived in their new countries with nothing, having been through great traumas and upheavals, and they built successful lives for themselves and for their families, often becoming extremely wealthy as a result of their labors. They worked harder and took greater risks than the indigenous populations that they were now living among, who had largely grown too comfortable and too risk-adverse to achieve the same levels of success. These are actually the people best equipped to make the necessary changes for the future.

It is reasonable to assume, therefore, that the great achievements of the future lie in the hands of the have-nots of today, as long as they are willing to rise up and think like revolutionaries and do not allow themselves to be persuaded to settle for incremental improvement and growth, and as long as their efforts are supported by those who have the finance and the political power to back them. For the sake of argument in this book, those have-nots also include the bulk of the younger generations, who in some cases are blocked from progressing with new and creative ideas by the older and more conservative generations, who are the ones controlling the purse strings which keep the capital from flowing to the places where it would be most likely to do the most good.

Whenever the repressed masses have come together and risen up in a well-organized fashion – as they have done from time to time over the centuries – they have often succeeded in overthrowing their perceived "masters," although always with terrible amounts of bloodshed and chaotic consequences for society (think of the fate of the rulers and aristocrats in both the French and the Russian revolutions, most of whom ended up being executed by the aggrieved masses).

These days, with modern communications, increased levels of education and new ways of consuming the news, it is a great deal easier to start a revolution – and to conclude it successfully, often without any physical bloodshed. This is an entirely healthy and natural process of renewal, evolution, and rebirth. If the older generations are going to be living longer, then they must accept that they need to hand over at least some of the power for creating change to the younger generations sooner than might have been the case in the past. It is, in fact, to their advantage to do so because it will increase prosperity for all of society, not just the young people themselves. Old people are naturally averse to change even though they will be the ones to benefit from it the most.

Radical change no longer has to lead to a civil war as the abolition of slavery did between the Northern and Southern US states, nor to battles on the streets as happened during the Civil Rights and Anti-War campaigns of the sixties. A supposedly "violent" backlash may now be marked by no more than a giant political rally or some aggressively noisy union picket lines; it might even happen entirely online, in the privacy of the revolutionaries' own smartphones.

There is always a danger, however, that if enough people feel sufficiently aggrieved with their situation, and do not feel they are able to make themselves heard any other way, then they will fall back into the traditional ways of readjusting the balance of power and undermining the ordered nature of society. It might be that this will come in the form of a cyberattack rather than a physical battle, but the results could be just as catastrophic. If, however, we think creatively enough we can avert that danger and bring the benefits of revolution to everyone without having to pay the price in blood or in the collapse of a vital element of our modern infrastructure.

Whenever the perceived gap between rich and poor grows too large and those on the wrong side of it become too disenchanted with their lives, the results can be destructive for everyone in the short term, even if they eventually produce ends that some say justify the means. Throughout history the wealth gaps have led to bloody uprisings, civil wars, and even the cold-bloodied execution or assassination of those who appear to possess an unfair proportion of the world's power and riches. In the West during the second half of the twentieth century, however, the gap remained relatively small for a variety of reasons. Blood has largely been spilled as a result of territorial or religious disputes rather than due to inequalities of wealth, and wars have been located mainly in parts of the world that possess large deposits of valuable raw materials, particularly oil.

> The answer cannot lie in slowing down progress or bringing down those who are doing well (i.e. the "hated rich" or the "billionaire classes"), although that often seems the easier option because it provides a scapegoat to blame for the problem and provides politicians with good sound bites. Instead it has to lie in bringing up the living standards of those who are in danger of being left behind.

In the twenty-first century, however, the globalized wealth gap is widening dangerously, which puts the already low paid out of work and benefits only a technologically sophisticated elite minority. It will continue to widen at ever-greater speed unless we do something radical and deliberate to slow it down and even, perhaps, to close it by speeding up the improvements for those who we are referring to as the have-nots.

This trend toward a widening gap is most obviously seen in the immense and sudden accumulation of wealth by technology companies in Silicon Valley and the rumblings of discontent around the world at how low the amounts of tax they appear to have to pay on their profits. This handful of corporations, however, has now grown so big and so wealthy that they are collectively worth more than many individual nations. It would be better, I feel, if they could be encouraged to direct their incredible wealth into the creation of new companies and new inventions, and in fairness they often are doing that. These famous giants, however, are only the most visible part of the iceberg. The same gaps and inequalities are opening up all over the world. It is now impossible to slow down the progress and growth of these companies without destroying the whole fabric of society, so it is imperative that we improve the lives of those people who keep the rest of the world economy turning over but do not get to share in the technology bonanza, and many of these trailblazing technocrats are already playing major roles in that process. Today's most successful trailblazers, such as Amazon, Google, Facebook, and Alibaba, are already starting the process of lifting everyone up.

What I am not saying is that the people who have created these companies should be vilified simply because their stock has become worth a great deal of money. Jeff Bezos is rich because he created Amazon, and the company has improved the lives of a great many of millions of customers; and Elon Musk is rich because he has invented an electric car that is likely to transform the way we all live in the coming decades. In many cases the individuals who created these colossally successful companies lead relatively simple personal lives, more interested in growing their companies than in reaping extravagant personal rewards. Mark Zuckerberg is famous for always wearing the same T-shirts and jeans, despite the fact that Facebook has, on paper, made him one of the richest men on the planet. It is far too easy for politicians to point fingers at these people and accuse them of being the problem, when in fact they are often the ones inventing the solutions. Where the inequality in earnings is less defensible is when executives who have created nothing, and who do not put their own money at risk, are hired to run the big companies and are paid millions of dollars simply for doing their jobs – or in some cases even paid millions of dollars for *not* doing their jobs.

It is much easier for politicians to blame the rich rather than doing the hard work of creating policies that will revolutionize the lives of those who feel they are being left behind. It is much easier to hurl abuse at the rich than to actually work out how to improve the lives of the poor.

For the sake of simplicity, we can say that there are currently around two and a half billion people on the planet who have more material goods, more opportunities, and more choices than at any time in history, and there are also five billion people on the other side of the wealth gap who are enjoying none of those benefits and whose lives appear to be getting worse in comparison, and sometimes in real terms as well. Many of the five billion have lifestyles which are infinitely better than their grandparents or great grandparents, but they do not feel that to be the case because they can see how wide the gap is between them and those who seem to be reaping the greatest rewards of progress.

As the chasm between the two and a half billion haves and the five billion have-nots grows wider, the potential for a destructive clash between the two sides increases, and it will take some radical and creative rethinking politically, socially, commercially, and financially to reverse the process and avert disaster. The world needs more creative entrepreneurs like Jeff Bezos, Mark Zuckerberg, and Jack Ma (Alibaba), not less.

Some would say that in order to close the gap we should limit the amount of money that the haves can control. When so much of the higher end of consumption is conspicuously flaunted by the media, it is bound to create dissatisfaction within the ranks of those who feel they will never be able to share in the good life that they see on their screens and in the shop windows they walk past. The system as it exists, however, has to flaunt its goods in this way in order to sell them. A large part of marketing and advertising is designed to make people feel that they want or need the products on display. Yet if those same people feel that they are never actually going to be able to have the products, it is not unreasonable for them to start to feel aggrieved and to resent the people they see enjoying the fruits of capitalist success without appearing to have done anything creative or taken any risks along the way.

The only viable solution is to radically lift the living standards and future prospects of the five billion have-nots so that they feel they are getting their fair share of the rewards of global progress and rising prosperity.

Some might think the only really feasible way to stop the rich acquiring an unfair share of the world's wealth is through more taxation, but effectively over-taxing the rich is proving impossible because if the rules change in one country the rich and enterprising simply move their money somewhere else or, worse still, stop working altogether. It is also an inadequate answer to the long-term problem because it cannot raise enough revenue to make any significant long-term difference to the lifestyles of the five billion on the other side of the gap. Nor does it solve the underlying problems of why five billion people are getting left behind in the first place and are starting to resent that fact.

That does not just mean that governments should simply hand out more free money; it also means increasing the opportunities and choices in every area of everyone's lives and increasing the amount of control they can exercise over their own destinies and on the world around them.

Feeling that you are being left behind financially is bad enough; feeling that you are helpless to do anything about it is far worse because that robs people of hope. We can all withstand a great deal if we are able to hope and believe that things are going to get better in the future.

During elections you hear politicians making promises of a better life if you just vote for them, but many of these promises would be entirely impossible to deliver on should they succeed in winning high office. Some of the great religions have been using this methodology for centuries, which might explain why they have been promising paradise and life after death for those who agree to tolerate poverty and servitude in this life. If you are told that however bad your life on earth might be you can be sure you will receive your reward in the afterlife, you are much more likely to stop complaining and to put up with the status quo. In extreme cases believers are even willing to go to war and face certain death in order to receive the rewards promised in the hereafter. I personally am quite spiritual and do believe in the afterlife, but that is not my point.

It is the hope of a better life on this side of the grave that drives most of the people who achieve great things. Someone who illegally crosses the Mexican border and is willing to work twelve hours a day in order to send money back to his or her family has to believe that by doing so they are building something better for their current and future generations. The same applies to Syrian refu-gees fleeing a war zone and young girls leaving the Philippines in order to work as nannies and chambermaids in the West. What they all have in common is hope that things will get easier and better for themselves and for their families.

Those in the West who have had no pay rise in ten years, however, or who have possibly seen the industry they and their ancestors have always worked in decline and disappear, have an entirely different view of the future and of the unfairness of life, even though their standards of living are far higher than most of the immigrants and refugees who are currently traveling the world in a state of hope. It is the people who find it hard to be hopeful whose revolutionary reactions result in the votes for Donald Trump and Brexit, while the immigrants and refugees are more likely to become creative revolutionaries, inventing new products and services and then working hard to make them a reality. It is no coincidence that most of the founding fathers of Hollywood were former refugees from Europe, people who arrived in New York and then trekked all the way to the wide-open spaces of California, filled with optimism about the industry they were going to create and with big dreams that became the stories they then sold back to the world.

The traditional wisdom has been that improvements in the lot of the poor are best done incrementally, day by day, month by month, year by year. It is the same principle as the one followed by established corporations when they are planning to increase their revenue and profits incrementally, a few percentage points each year. Conservative by nature, because they have a lot to protect, established corporations try to generate new profits without endangering their existing sources of income – often by simply cutting costs and shrinking their workforces rather than being bold and trying out new initiatives or creating new businesses. Conservative, cautious, and incremental approaches to closing the wealth gap are inevitably going to be just as counterproductive, especially in a world that is undergoing a power shift.

As Geoffrey West puts it in his excellent book, *Scale*, published in 2017, "As they grow companies tend to become more and more unidimensional, driven partly by market forces but also by the inevitable ossification of the top-down administrative and bureaucratic needs perceived as necessary for operating a traditional company in the modern era." He goes on to explain that "change, adaptation, and reinvention become increasingly difficult to effect, especially as the external socioeconomic clock is continually accelerating and conditions change at a faster and faster rate."

In other words, events are moving too fast now for that sort of unimaginative, risk-averse behavior to be an effective solution any longer. Incremental change may buy you some time, whether you are a politician or a CEO.

It may keep you afloat in the short term, but it will not save you from ultimate extinction – and it will never change the world. Time never loses the war.

The gap between the haves and the have-nots, however, is not the only division opening up in society. In many Western countries the idea of political consensus, and of people from different parties working together for the common good, is being eroded to a far greater extent than it has been in any living memory. Clashes mainly seem to come from the far right and the far left, the middle ground having been hollowed out and the media having provoked and stirred up controversy wherever they can, knowing that it is controversy which gets people's attention and consequently increases the value of the advertising space that surrounds the alarmist and confrontational stories being told.

Nowhere is this more noticeable than in the United States in 2017. You only have to look at the record of George Bush Senior, who was president between 1989 and 1993, after serving as a congressman, vice president, and director of the CIA, to see how much things have changed. He was a Republican congressman under both Democratic and Republican presidents, and in both cases, he voted virtually the same percentage of times with the incumbent president, following his own conscience regardless of party. That meant that half the time he was not voting with his party. Now everyone in Congress votes at least 90 percent of the time with their party rather than their conscience and the idea of everyone working together for one America seems to have disappeared over a relatively short period of time.

■ Pick ideas not sides. Ideas don't win or lose, sides do.

When America was founded – by a revolution – Britain was in the middle of a great deal of political upheaval. It had a heavy burden of national debt and huge pressure on national spending. There was popular unrest everywhere and real religious conflict. During that time Britain lost the American colonies and exactly the same set of circumstances are now occurring within the United States. We see no respectful disagreement between different sides, just name-calling, personal contempt, hatred, labeling, and the public humiliation of people with differing views.

We are seeing an increasing contempt for authority, especially public authority. We are seeing a populism that is blind to the facts on both sides, and we are seeing destruction of personal property on the rise. We see politicians using words to motivate and inspire followers but making no effort to enlighten or teach them the real facts. In order to ensure that it does not experience a similar loss of power and influence in the world as Britain, America needs to face reality, listen to and accept opposing views, and discuss them constructively, and get out of the echo chamber of social media.

The public has grown tired of watching politicians behaving like children, which is possibly another of the reasons why they protested by making Donald Trump, a non-politician, president. Likewise, in France the public decided that Emmanuel Macron, a young ex-banker, should be made president rather than choosing a career politician. We don't, at the time of writing this, know how these decisions will pan out, but it is my suspicion that neither of them is going to be able to solve the core problem, although I hope I am wrong.

The chances of being able to heal these political divides naturally or in the near future are low. The only solution in America is probably to blow up the two-party model and create a third, independent party, which will force the political elite to go back to behaving like adults. So, in politics as in business, only blowing up the model can make the necessary changes happen.

As well as being the right thing to do, blowing up the model is also a great deal more fun for those who are planning and executing the revolution, requiring us to be both creative and imaginative. But it is only fun for as long as we do it right. Nothing is worse than a revolution which fails to gain traction and ends up with the leaders of the uprising being locked away for the rest of their lives or, worse still, stood up against a wall and shot. (The sort of revolutions I am going to be talking about in this book will not, of course, have such drastic outcomes should they fail, but still it is never fun to lose.)

Those with vested interests in the status quo will always fight to protect what they have, partly out of fear of losing it and also out of laziness, because it is always easier to keep doing what you have been doing for years and to leave the problems of the future for later generations to solve, than to overturn the model and start doing things differently.

So, anyone wanting to blow up the model and start a revolution has to accept that they are going to have to fight against those who believe in the established way of doing things, and these people make for powerful enemies because they are also the people who have been running things for a long time. They created the modern world that we live in and so they are unlikely to want to see it blown up.

Anyone wanting things to get better, however, needs to be starting to plan their own revolution today.

- Think of all the things that you believe should be different, both in your own life and in the world around you, but which you believe are impossible to change.
- Visualize the future that you want for yourself and your family.

3

When the Revolutionaries Become the Establishment and Stop Blowing Up the Model

"Ever tried. Ever failed. No matter. Try again. Fail again. Fail Better."
—Samuel Beckett

I have always been fascinated by individuals who are able to motivate millions of people to take on causes and to go headlong into battles that they know might lead to them being killed. The skills of persuasion needed to achieve that are enormous. We in the West are puzzled by the young suicide bombers who are willing to blow themselves to pieces for a religious cause, yet many millions of soldiers over the centuries have been equally willing to take almost as great a risk. The troops who went over the top of the French trenches of the First World War soon learned that the odds of survival were low, but they still believed they should do as they were told. The Japanese pilots who deliberately flew their planes into ships were equally willing to give their lives for the cause they had been told was worth dying for (nearly four thousand of them died that way in the Second World War).

21

A movement that starts with one charismatic person – it could be Adolf Hitler or Nelson Mandela, Gandhi or Saddam Hussein, Kim Jong-un or Chairman Mao, Fidel Castro or Pol Pot – can grow powerful enough to topple a whole government, lead a country into war or into committing genocide, and can change the course of civilization as a result. Just as some of these game changers can do great amounts of damage, other exceptional individuals can achieve great, positive strides forward by standing up to conventional thinking and being certain there are better ways of doing things – we could be talking about Albert Einstein or Steve Jobs, Thomas Edison or Galileo Galilei, Henry Ford or Golda Meir, Jack Ma or Arthur Guinness, Muhammad Ali or Rosa Parks – despite being lone voices at the start of their careers. I find the whole "David versus Goliath" story deeply inspiring and always have.

I believe that all of us are capable of achieving far more than we believe possible, but we only find that out when we are pushed to what we pre-viously believed were the limits of our abilities. There is a famous cliché, "necessity is the mother of invention," which, like most clichés, is undoubt-edly true. When people believe their lives, or the lives of those they love, depend on it, they are capable of achieving incredible things. When the Sec-ond World War broke out, productivity in US car factories went up around 400 percent because they stopped producing recreational cars and started producing military vehicles. Not only that, they were also building tanks and bombs and bullets at the same time, and this was at a time when most of the skilled and able-bodied workforce had been sent overseas to fight. The majority of the work was being carried out by newly recruited women who had no previous experience in heavy industry. Until it was called upon, all that latent energy had been lying dormant, waiting to be released. Latent energy is always there, and leaders just need to be able to find the key to unlock this potential and motivate people to be creative in their thinking and diligent in the execution of their ideas in order to transform the future.

The neuroscientists tell us that we use only a tiny proportion of our brains' capacity, and we all know that we utilize only a tiny proportion of the power which now lies within our computers and smartphones. It is the same with human potential. The vast majority of human potential lies untapped most of the time. Just imagine what we could achieve together if we were able to access it with the help of technology and artificial intelligence.

I had a personal assistant for more than twenty years called Blair, who has now gone on to become a life coach. "I learned from you that it is possible to push people to do things they never dreamed they were capable of," she told me recently. "You have no idea how many people would come out of your office after you had told them to go and do something they had never done before, like produce a kids' show or start a new company, and ask me how on earth they were supposed to do that. I'd tell them that they should definitely not go back in and ask you because you would simply give the job to someone else. So they had to pull on their grown-up pants and have a go. If it didn't come out right, we could all figure it out later. I did that so many times, and now, as a life coach, I do the same for people who don't have a boss like you who's pushing them to achieve more and get to their God-given human potential."

I always expected people to do things they had previously believed impossible. I always wanted them to think like revolutionaries and come up with completely new ideas that would change everything that had come before. The New Jersey *Star-Ledger* once called me "Che Guevara in a nice suit," and I took that as a compliment. I would like to think that I am a revolutionary, despite the fact that to the five billion have-nots we are talking about, the ones who reside on the wrong side of the wealth gap, I would appear to be firmly in among the two and a half billion. But then most of the people who currently sit at the top of the wealth pile started out as outsiders, lone voices in the wilderness.

It's not hard to talk bravely about disrupting the status quo. Anyone can dream of overturning the system and replacing it with something better. In fact, I suspect most young people dream of doing something like that at some time in their lives.

> The trick is to remain entrepreneurial and revolutionary once you have achieved that goal and once you are sitting safely on the comfortable side of the wealth gap.

The new giants of the corporate world such as Apple, Google, Facebook, Alibaba, and Amazon were all started by entrepreneurs who behaved like revolutionaries. They "blew up the model," destroying old ways of doing things in the process. None of these founders came from the poorest end of the spectrum, although much is made of the fact that Steve Jobs, who founded Apple, was "the son of a Syrian immigrant," but they were still outsiders in that they were not people who could be absorbed easily by the corporate world until they had performed their acts of revolution and taken control of the new models they were building. They inevitably started as outsiders because it would have been impossible for these men and their creations to emerge from inside major corporations. Major corporations simply cannot afford to think like revolutionaries, which is why they are all destined to fail in the end, however big they may be. No one is ever really "too big to fail" – that phrase was invented by politicians to explain why they wanted to rescue the banks when the whole system came close to collapse in 2008.

Coming up behind those famous giants there is another generation of revolutionaries, who have started companies like Uber and Airbnb, and the money-lending apps in Africa. These people have used crowdsourcing to upset the status quo of business models that have existed for centuries. In the cases of Uber and Airbnb those models of the status quo would be the cab companies that have worked to roughly the same business model since they were operating horse-drawn carriages, and the hotel industry, which has also worked to a largely unchanged business model for centuries. In the case of the money-lending apps in Africa, it is the traditional money-lenders who are being replaced by a more democratic model. The big banks did not want to find a way to serve the underserved, so the people invented their own way. Again, we see a revolution starting from the bottom. When regulators get around to allowing data portability, so that customers can move more easily to new apps and services, there will be another revolution.

At the time of writing this, these companies are still controversial and it is uncertain what the next stages of their evolution will be, but the trend toward crowdsourcing is a major contributor to the current wave of revolutions which are upsetting the existing models, a trend that was made possible by the work of the previous generation of entrepreneurs at Apple, Google, Facebook, Alibaba, and Amazon. These giants, however, although they are still young enough to be adept at adapting the ways they operate in order to meet changing market conditions, are already too big and unwieldy to be true revolutionaries any longer. They are now so huge it is inevitable that they will become the models that a future generation will eventually find ways to disrupt and rethink.

Just as a grown man or woman who dresses like a teenager and behaves in delinquent ways will often appear deluded and foolish, big companies cannot easily return to the ways of their revolutionary early days, however much they may want to. They have moved on to the next stage in their evolution and it is time for new minds and new ideas to come along and start chipping away at their position. This is a natural cycle.

Big businesses all eventually behave in the same way; they all become risk-adverse and they all start looking for ways to preserve the status quo, to consolidate their positions against competitors, and preserve their existing markets by cutting jobs and replacing their workforces with automation once the phenomenal growth rates of their early years start to slow down.

In his 2016 letter to shareholders, Amazon's founder and CEO, Jeff Bezos, outlined exactly this problem, defining it as being the difference between "Day One," when a company starts out with all the sharpness of an entrepreneurial venture, and "Day Two," when it starts to mature. Day Two, he warned, could mean "stasis, followed by irrelevance, followed by excruciating, painful decline. Followed by death."

That, he said, was why the company had to maintain "Day One vitality" forever. To do that Amazon had to concentrate on "defense, customer obsession, a skeptical view of proxies" (such as situations where the process or market research or customer surveys become the thing which drives everything else), "the eager adoption of external trends and" – most important of all in my opinion – "high velocity decision making." He went on to say that the company needed to "experiment patiently, accept failures, plant seeds, protect saplings, and double down when you see customer delight. . .If you won't or can't embrace powerful trends quickly, if you fight them, you're probably fighting the future. Embrace them and you have a tailwind."

Eighty percent of the new jobs created in any one year in America come from start-ups and small businesses. The same applies to the new inventions that appeal the most to vast proportions of the world's population.

While big, established businesses almost inevitably look for ways to decrease the number of people they need to hire in order to cut costs, the newer, smaller businesses have to take a very different approach to risk, and consequently they are the ones that are creating new jobs as they thrive and grow, filled with hope and optimism for their future.

It is the people who sell cars to a world that previously only had horses, television sets to people who previously relied on the radio for home entertainment, or mobile phones to people who previously had only landlines, who revolutionize marketplaces, create entirely new industries, and change the way that everyone lives almost overnight. It is the new companies and the new ideas that generate the real growth, while the giants of yesterday can only increase their size by stealing one another's market shares and end up pouring all their energy into mergers and acquisitions, just to keep growing, just to stay alive a few years longer, like geriatrics reliant on pharmaceuticals for their vitality and continued existence.

The biggest opportunities always belong to entrepreneurs who can think and act big and creatively. The great start-ups are never born within large companies. They happen in someone's garage, like Apple, or in college, as with Facebook. Microsoft wasn't born in the laboratories of IBM but in Albuquerque when Bill Gates took a leave of absence from Harvard and teamed up with Paul Allen. Large companies can never move as swiftly as entrepreneurs because they are tied down with overhead, brand reputations, and regulations. They have gigantic markets to protect so they can't afford to take the same risks as the woman or man starting out on their own, just as individuals become less comfortable taking big risks once they are married with children, mortgages, and other responsibilities. This is not bad; it is just the reality of life.

It wasn't the guy in the oil lamp business who invented the light bulb and it wasn't the horse and buggy guy who invented the automobile. These sorts of revolutionary moves forward have to be made by outsiders, by revolutionaries attacking the citadels of the big corporations.

The same rules apply to the individuals who work at senior levels within big companies. If you are an executive and you head up a department of 200 people, which you can see no longer adds anything positive to the company, and you realize that the right and brave thing to do would be to blow up the department, get rid of those 200 people and do things completely differently, you are unlikely to act upon that realization for reasons of self-interest. People become less and less inclined to behave like revolutionaries as they move up the corporate ladder and have more to lose. An entrepreneur, however, whose life and soul are entwined in the success of their company, is more likely to be willing to take the more disruptive route to success, because they understand that often that is also the only route to survival. If you have been in a company for a long time it is pleasant to have 200 people working for you. It is uncomfortable to think that you might have to start from scratch again, that you might lose your status and might have to do things differently and learn new skills – maybe even find a new job. So the chances are that you will not voice your opinion that rethinking the model would be the best thing for the future of the company as a whole. Better also to silence anyone else who might express the view that things need to change.

From the point of view of the more creative people working inside the big corporations, however, it is always more exciting to be working with someone who is blowing up the model. Just ask yourself the question: Would it be more exciting to go into work each day at Amazon (who are still revolutionaries despite their size), where they are working out how to deliver packages all over the world by drone or at Coca-Cola, where they are working out how to take a few percentage points of sugar out of a fizzy drink that has been on the market for more than 100 years? Would you rather be working on the first driverless cars or virtual reality headsets at Google's Moonshot Factory at X company, or trying to cut office overheads at one of the big clearing banks? When Jack Welch was CEO of General Electric, the stock value went up 4,000 percent in 20 years. The company grew from $12 billion to $280 billion as a result, among other things, of his decision to shift into emerging markets. He also cut the number of people the company was employing by more than a hundred thousand in five years. He left in 2001, around the time of the dot-com bust, and at the time of writing this, GE stock has not moved for 17 years. Soon after he left the company, I wrote him a letter saying that I would like to come and see him. I received back a standard typed letter of rejection, but down the side he had written "standard," and at the bottom was a hand-written note inviting me to visit him in his office.

I duly called him, and he invited me in to his office in Rockefeller Center, very generously giving me a day of his time. I didn't want to waste a second of it, so I asked him to walk me through all the big things he had learned in his business career, such as when you do reviews with people do them in person, but put them in writing afterward because people will only remember the positives and never remember the negatives unless they see them in writing.

"Once you've figured out your mission," he told me, "repeat it a thousand times. Over and over again. Don't think that just because you have said it ten times that everyone in the company gets it. Use a sledgehammer if you have to."

"Separate your strategy meetings from your operational meetings," was another bit of advice, "because otherwise everyone will want to talk about all the bullshit strategy stuff that is exciting to talk about instead of talking about the nuts and bolts of operations."

Jack also believed you should be disciplined and get rid of the bottom 10 percent of your employees each year. "They may not think it," he said, "but you are doing them a favor because if they are not doing well with you, they need to move on.

"The other mistake people make is putting whoever is available onto new projects. But the people who are 'available' are usually the people who are proving least useful elsewhere. What you should do is pull all your best people off whatever they are doing and put them on the new project. If the other parts of the business are strong, they will survive without those people. They may not want to leave what they are doing to move to a start-up, but if they are good, they will embrace the challenge and they will grow it into something big. If you take whoever is 'available' the project will never succeed."

I asked Jack what he thought his successor, Jeffrey Immelt, should do. "He has a healthy stock," Jack said. "He should buy every relevant business he can with that stock."

If Jeffrey had done that, he could have bought all sorts of interesting cash flow and opportunities; as it is the company has remained entirely stationary, as if waiting for death to come. Hopefully Jeffrey's successor will find a way to blow up the model.

Years after I first met Jack, Jimmy Lee, the vice-chairman at J.P. Morgan, invited us both to come and talk to his senior executives about "bumps in the road," meaning how to recover from setbacks in your career. My message was that whatever happens, you always need to take care of your partners in a business venture because then you will be able to go back to them with your next idea and they will still be willing to work with you.

This was after we had been caught out with six billion dollars of debt. I had just sent a check for a billion dollars plus interest to the CEO of J.P. Morgan and he had written me a letter saying that none of the other dot-com start-ups they had funded had paid them back in full. It had been Jimmy Lee who had advised me to do that.

"When most people get in trouble, they never pay their bank back," Jimmy had told me, "but you should make them your priority."

It was good advice because twenty years later I am still working with all the people who were involved in that disastrous deal.

Building good relations with business partners can pay off in all sorts of unexpected ways. Launny Steffens was vice-chairman of Merrill Lynch, and I met him when I opened up an account there. We were doing a lot of work with them at that stage, taking full-page ads together in the business media. One day I changed brokers and when they transferred my files there was a mistake that resulted in my credit card being turned down by a vendor. I called up Launny to tell him.

"I've personally adjusted your account," he assured me. "It will never happen again."

"What do I do if it does happen?" I asked.

"If it does happen again get the vendor concerned to call me up on my personal number and I'll pay the bill."

A year later I was celebrating some deal with my team, because I'm a great believer in always celebrating your successes (it was one of the ten tips that Jack Welch gave me), at Bravo Gianni restaurant in New York, somewhere I frequented for twenty years. It was a great place, where you might easily see Rupert Murdoch sitting in one corner; a mafia boss in another corner; and Don King, the boxing promoter, in another. My credit card failed again so I gave Launny Steffens's home number to Gianni and told him to call, even though it was by then the middle of the night.

"He's vice-chairman of Merrill Lynch," I explained. "He'll take care of it."

Gianni picked up the phone on the bar and dialed the number.

"Hey, Mister Launny," Gianni growled in his thick Italian accent when Launny's sleepy voice answered, "this is Gianni, you have a problem."

Launny was good to his word and took care of what I'm sure was a $3,000 tab. I had other credit cards in my pocket, but it was too much fun to watch Gianni make the call.

I have often wondered why Jack Welch invited me in that day. It's not the only time that someone has surprised me in that way. Why do people agree to give their time and advice to some people and not to others? Is it because they like them? Is it because they want something from them? Is it because they have a worthy cause? Or is it simply because you asked, and not many people actually have the nerve to do that? In truth it's probably a mixture of all those, but you can be sure that if you don't ask for help you won't get anywhere. Throughout this book you will find many examples of people who have helped me. Without that help my career would not have been possible. So, surround yourself with people like Launny Steffens, who would rather cut off a finger than not live up to their word.

So it is the creative young revolutionaries who create prosperity and growth, while the apparently wealthy old dinosaurs expend all their energies on simply staying alive. It is the creative thinkers and risk-takers who should be helped and encouraged by the tax system and investment infrastructure. If, for instance, the tax system were to be designed to encourage entrepreneurial thinking it would inevitably lead to a rise in employment figures, radical improvements in the products and services available to everyone, falling prices, rising living standards, and gains for everyone. This would help the bottom five billion.

I believe that anyone who makes money simply as a passive investor, merely buying stock in a big company and selling it at a profit, should be taxed on that profit. But the situation should be different if someone is selling a company they have created from nothing and built themselves in order to invest the money in a bigger idea which will become a company that employs more people and creates more wealth. It is at this stage of the business cycle that wealth and employment can be generated to the benefit of the whole community, and entrepreneurs should be encouraged to invest in new companies all the time and assisted wherever possible. If a landscape gardener, for instance, wants to sell her business in order to invest in a larger fertilizer business because she has spotted a gap in the market, she should receive some sort of tax advantage on the money she gains on selling her first company, in this case the landscaping business, provided it is invested in the new company, bearing in mind that 80 percent of new jobs are created by small companies.

In other words, she should be encouraged to use that money to build a new company which will create jobs rather than simply taking the money and putting it in the bank or buying a yacht. The employees in her new fertilizer company will then be able to pay tax and contribute to the general good of the nation on an ongoing basis. If you overtax the landscape gardener when she sells her business, the taxman only receives a one-off windfall and there is no repeat tax income and less potential for growth for the future. The whole financial system should be geared to encouraging growth and creativity in order to provide benefits for all. Many of the greatest investors and entrepreneurs continue creating companies well into their eighties and nineties, providing huge amounts of employment and many opportunities for wealth creation that add to the collective good.

- When you are deciding where to channel your efforts look for new ideas, young people, and start-ups. They are the giants of tomorrow.
- If you choose instead to go to the places where the established giants already rule, then you are investing your life in something which is inevitably in decline, even if it is not yet evident.

4

Entrepreneurial Thinkers Can Be Found in Every Walk of Life

"Start by doing what's necessary; then do what's possible; and suddenly you are doing the impossible."

—*St. Francis of Assisi*

People who think creatively like revolutionaries are in the minority, but they can be found in every walk of life, not just as entrepreneurs in start-up businesses or as warriors in political battles.

Einstein, for instance, was a revolutionary because he refused to believe that things weren't different to how everyone had perceived them up till then, and as a result he changed our understanding of relativity, time, and space. His farsightedness also had very practical results, which changed the way the world ended up after the Second World War. He wrote to President Roosevelt soon after arriving in the United States to warn that the Germans were on the verge of inventing a nuclear weapon and that if the Allies didn't beat them to it the whole game would be over very quickly and wouldn't end well. If the Germans were already killing people in the millions, it was not hard to predict what damage they would have been willing to inflict with an atomic bomb.

Just sending that letter demonstrated entrepreneurial thinking: Einstein was looking into a possible future where all the rules of combat would change in ways that were still impossible for most people to grasp and then working out how things might play out in order for mankind to reach that scenario. "I know not," he famously said, "with what weapons World War III will be fought, but World War IV will be fought with sticks and stones."

It was unusual for a physicist to be able to think like that and to be able to actually take action on those thoughts. Most people would not have seen the danger, and most who were able to see it would have thought it was too big a problem for them to be able to take any sort of useful action to solve it.

Like Einstein, we need to apply the same principles of revolutionary entrepreneurship to every sphere of our lives, including politics, religion, diplomacy, education, taxation, wealth distribution, the swelling refugee crisis, employment, automation, healthcare, climate change, terrorism, and technology. This is by no means an exclusive list because the same principles apply to everything in our world that we currently have any control over or care about, but it gives an idea of the breadth of the potential for changing things for the better. Everyone could revolutionize their lives and the lives of those around them if they learn to think creatively. We must not be afraid to think big or to ask for help; we must ask questions and really listen to the answers.

Nothing should be considered too sacred or too big to be reinvented. The Roman Catholic Church is a particularly good example of a model that is in need of a rethink but is believed by many to be untouchable. If anyone can do this, it is the current pope. He is doing a lot to help the changes come, by simplifying his own life, living and eating with everyone else in the Vatican, helping the poor, and leading by example, but it will probably need more than one man, no matter how talented, to rethink a model this big and this old. As a member of the Catholic Church and, I believe, a good Christian, how can I not support the concept of priests marrying, especially as they are required to give marriage advice to young couples? How could I not support the ordaining of female priests, the half of the population that, in my experience, are generally the better listeners, when listening is a major part of a priest's job? How can I not support the use of contraception, especially in parts of the world where they struggle to feed their children and where sexually transmitted diseases are rampant?

The Church was originally created in an entirely different time in order to meet the needs of people who lived entirely different lives to those we live today and who believed many different things about the world. As an institution it is so huge and so old, however, with so many vested interests, that it's never going to volunteer itself to be blown up. Rather, it will keep trying to improve and modernize itself with small incremental changes while all the time its power and credibility gradually seep away. It will be a long time before it is entirely gone, simply because it is so enormous, so ancient, and so deeply rooted in society, but an end is possible and even foreseeable unless it reinvents itself from top to bottom, particularly when it comes to matters where it seems so out of step with the views of the general population, such as contraception, recruiting female priests, and allowing all priests to marry. Nothing lasts forever, however much we might wish the contrary to be true.

Everything has a natural lifespan and a cycle of growth and decline or, if you prefer, evolution. The former president of Ireland, Mary McAleese, went on to study for a doctorate in Canon Law. She recently explained to me that Canon Law states that if the flock no longer embraces a teaching or doctrine of the Church, it brings into question the validity and integrity of that teaching or doctrine.

All over the world power is shifting toward populism at every level of society. This is mainly due to better forms of personal communication, the growing accessibility of big data through connectivity and social media, and an increased awareness among the bulk of the population of what is happening in the world. Much of this has been caused by media exposure in areas of established authority that were previously hidden from the rest of us by interested and powerful parties (i.e. the various "Establishments"). The speeding up of globalization has also speeded up the processes of disintermediation in every industry, cutting out the middlemen at every level in order to maintain a competitive edge.

The age of automatic deference to authority has passed in many parts of the world, and people are now able to talk directly to one another without having to go through a third party like the media. Probably the most dramatic examples of this were the birth of WikiLeaks and the amount of information people like Edward Snowden were willing to leak to them, but the trend toward transparency had been growing long before that through newspaper exposés of politicians, royal families, and business leaders, and through reality television shows which showed what was going on behind doors that had previously been closed.

There is often a spell that needs to be broken before people are able to see and realize their own potential. When Mike Tyson was world heavyweight boxing champion, he was famous for always knocking his opponents out in the first or second rounds. His opponents consequently fought defensively simply to avoid that happening to them, until a virtual unknown succeeded in knocking Tyson out and the spell was broken. The other fighters were able to see that he was not invincible and that they did stand a chance against him, and his unbroken record of victories was over.

As a result of this growing transparency, largely due to the openness of the internet and other media, entrepreneurial thinking can be seen emerging in some of the most unlikely places, places that previously were thought of as "unchanging," their existing traditions and rules "written in stone." The time when people were willing to accept that those in positions of authority were automatically right in everything they said and did, and should be respected simply because of their positions, is now over. Priests were once believed to be the fonts of all wisdom and doctors expected patients to accept all their pronouncements without question. Not anymore. We now know that they, as well as teachers and cops, have the same flaws as the rest of us. There are negative consequences as well, such as the difficulties that teachers can face with students who do not want to learn and do not accept discipline, but on the whole it is a positive development for humanity.

The transformations can be seen most dramatically in political events such as the election of Donald Trump to the US presidency and the British electorate voting to leave the European Union. Both were almost universally considered to be impossible until the final moment, when they became realities. There were also the events that came to be known collectively as the "Arab Spring," which started in Tunisia in 2010 and spread throughout the Middle Eastern region and which would previously have been considered impossible.

With the election of Trump (and to a degree President Obama before him), and the first mass rallies of the Arab Spring, it was the clever use of social media which made it possible to achieve political results in new ways. Once he was in office, President Trump continued to make use of the new media to develop his power base in ways that would previously have been considered inappropriate for the holder of such an elite and powerful position. However, because he is, according to White House officials, undisciplined, he gives the impression that he doesn't care too much about policy or about understanding the issues. This apparent openness may also be his undoing. He took the idea of "transparency" to a whole new level. People were able to hear and read exactly what he was thinking and what he wanted them to know he was doing, by following him on Twitter. They were also able to see his faults more clearly. It allowed ordinary people to feel that they had a direct relationship with the man, but it also stripped away much of the traditional mystery and magic of leadership. It is a genie that the traditional Establishment, those who have been in power for the last few centuries, will probably never be able to get back into the bottle now that it has been released.

A similar pulling back of the curtain occurred when the British royal family first allowed film cameras inside their private lives in 1969, albeit under the controlled and respectful conditions which still prevailed at that time. Many traditionalists believed that the mystique had been destroyed forever, but it is also possible that it was by showing themselves to be normal people, albeit living abnormal lives, the family has managed to stay on their thrones for far longer than any other modern monarchs.

When Toto, the dog in *The Wizard of Oz,* pulls back the curtain and Dorothy discovers that the Wizard, who had seemed so powerful and fearsome, is actually a normal middle-aged man who has simply been projecting the fearsome image onto a screen, the Wizard instantly loses all his power to rule by fear. But, by ruling with love, concern, and understanding instead, he is nevertheless able to deliver a happy ending for Dorothy and her fellow travelers.

In much the same way, in the twenty-first century, a concept which has been named "populism" has risen up to challenge perceived political elitism all over the world, and disintermediation has dramatically altered the way businesses function, forcing the new generation of entrepreneurs to invent new ways to be successful. The closer the business decisions are to the customer (like President Trump and his Twitter followers), the more likely that they are going to be popular with their chosen audiences (although obviously not with everyone) and effective. Decision-makers who are buried away inside corporate structures (like traditional royal families and wizards locked inside palaces) are far less likely to be in touch with the realities of the marketplace, or to be thinking creatively or in a revolutionary way, or to be taking the appropriate risks needed to make quantum, game-changing leaps forward.

Governments, populations, and businesses that do not rethink the model and reinvent themselves are destined to eventually fail, resulting in lost jobs, lost wealth, lost health, lost happiness, lost security and lost opportunities. Responsibility for turning things around does not lie solely on the shoulders of the business world or on our political leaders; it belongs to all of us. To make the most of the opportunities that the changes in the power structure are creating, and to avoid the chaos that will result if we continue to react too slowly and too unimaginatively to our changing circumstances, we must all revolutionize the way we think and the way we behave in all areas of our lives in order to be more creatively entrepreneurial.

- Do not restrict your creative thinking simply to your business or your career. Treat it as a holistic concept, covering every part of your life and the lives of all those that you might be able to touch in a positive way.
- Do not assume that those who currently control things will continue to do so. It is possible that your ideas are better than theirs.

5

Can You Teach Entrepreneurship or are Creative Entrepreneurs Born that Way?

"Times and conditions change so rapidly that we must keep our aim constantly focused on the future."

—Walt Disney

All the top schools and universities around the world now have courses in "entrepreneurship." It is a fashionable subject, and if you ask them why they have added it to the curriculum, they will tell you it's because the students are "insisting on it."

If you ask the students to honestly say why they want to be entrepreneurs they will most often say it's because they want to be "rich" and because they "don't want to have a boss." But no high-quality entrepreneur I have ever met has chosen that path in order to get rich, and if you ask them they will all tell you that they have had a boss or a mentor who has helped them along the way. No one succeeds at anything without the support of others.

So the two things the young people who enroll at the schools and universities are trying to accomplish and avoid are the opposite of the motivation that is actually needed in order to become a great creative entrepreneur. What many of the students are actually saying is that they are hoping the course will show them ways to avoid having to get a job – an altogether less creative ambition.

The students, however, are the customers in this situation, so it's a good thing for the schools to listen to what they want and to react to it in order to provide the courses that will be popular. At the same time, these students are, by and large, teenagers, who are not yet worldly enough to really understand what it is they are asking for. They still need at least some guidance in their life choices, even if they do not believe that to be the case at the time.

The other point that I would like to make, and frequently do whenever I have the ear of one of the deans, is that if the universities really believed in the value of entrepreneurial behavior it would be endemic across their campuses, not just contained within the books and lecture halls or in one course. In my considerable experience, however, that is almost never the case. The thinking, therefore, behind the "teaching" of entrepreneurship is seldom pure. If they really believed in entrepreneurship it wouldn't just be contained in the business schools, it would also be found in the medical schools, the law schools, and the schools of foreign service. The laws of tort, for instance, need complete rethinking to make them effective in the modern world, and diplomats need training in how to think creatively far more urgently than business people, most of whom will be able to figure out how to make money sooner or later, whether they have university degrees or not. What we are talking about here is the difficult intersection between creativity, entrepreneurship, and effective execution, which is a tough trifecta to get right.

I'm pretty sure that I was born a creative entrepreneur. I was the youngest of seven siblings, living with my parents in Watertown, a suburb of Boston and the second biggest industrial town in America, in the 1950s and 1960s. My first entrepreneurial challenge was probably working out how to get into the one bathroom shared by nine of us. My mother's parents, the Brodericks, lived in their own little house out the back of ours, making eleven of us in all. My father's mother, sister, brother, and sister-in-law all lived close to one another as well, but in another town.

Sitting next to President Reagan at dinner that time I mentioned earlier, I noticed the president had light stubble on his chin, like he hadn't shaved that morning, which surprised me at the time. Later I read in his autobiography that he always showered, shaved, and laid out his suit late at night, before going to bed, instead of in the morning, which is what my father, a man of meticulous habit, always used to do. I guess it was a custom that came from times when most men did manual labor during the day and wanted to clean themselves up before going to bed with their wives, but I wonder now if in my dad's case it also had something to do with finding a moment when he could get to spend some time in the only bathroom we had.

My mother's father, John, we all called "Daddy John" because he had taken over the role of family patriarch during the years when my father was away at war. Apparently, my siblings had taken to calling him "Dad," and so when our real father returned, Mom suggested that we called her father "Daddy John" instead, so as not to offend my dad.

When Germany surrendered, my father was one of the first Allied soldiers to enter Hitler's Eagle's Nest, and he brought back the silk flag from behind the Führer's desk as a trophy. After he died, we donated it to the CIA Cold War Museum.

My mother's mother had come over from Ireland using someone else's ticket when she was just sixteen. Her friend had bought a ticket but got sick and couldn't travel, so my grandmother made an instant decision and took her place, leaving one week later, which seems like an incredibly brave thing for such a young girl to do. If she had decided not to take that gamble everything would have been different. That one decision by my grandmother, to take the ticket, set in motion all the events that would become my life.

Because both her parents had made the same journey, my mother had no grandparents in America, the rest of her family having all stayed behind in Ireland. My mother was their only child – I believe because the midwife had caused my grandmother so much damage, she was never able to conceive again – so she had no siblings either. Her husband, children, and grandchildren would become her entire family, with her firmly at the center.

Her father, my maternal grandfather, was the most Irish of men, growing his own food, canning his own vegetables in the basement, and never driving a car. He worked first as a janitor and then a streetcar driver. He too had come over to America from Ireland, which must have been an uncomfortable 3,000-mile sea trip into the unknown. When he arrived, he was carrying one steamer trunk, which contained every single thing he owned. I have it on display in my house, using it as a coffee table, just to remind my kids that their great-grandfather started a whole new life in a new country with a case that is smaller than something they would take away for the weekend.

My dad's family was also from Ireland. He was a civil contractor, as his dad and his grandfather had been before him (his grandfather, John McCourt, having been the one to bring the family across the Atlantic), specializing in roads, sidewalks, runways, and utilities, never building anything more than three feet above the ground and seldom more than three feet below. The job Dad took the most pride in was the runway he built at Logan International Airport. If we had a guest coming for the weekend, Dad would always volunteer to pick them up at the airport. That came with the price of a full tour of everything he had built there, and, by the end of his career, that included just about every runway and taxiway.

It is in the stories of men like John Broderick, my maternal grandfather, and John McCourt, my paternal great-grandfather, that the seeds of true entrepreneurship lay. As I have already mentioned, their generations sailed from the home country of their ancestors to escape poverty and to search for opportunities, much as today's immigrants from Africa and the Middle East are doing, although sometimes they are escaping the even more immediate dangers of political persecution, bombs, and executions, just as the Jewish diaspora has been forced to do many times in many different countries over the centuries.

In almost all cases, people who, like Daddy John and John McCourt, have the courage and foresight to leave a familiar but bad situation and set out into an unknown foreign world in search of something better, are the ones who achieve great things, create great things, and move mankind forward. Some six million people left Ireland for America in that period, but unlike the immigrants of today, they had time to make a clear decision and lay plans for building a better future for themselves and for the country they were going to. It was still a great leap into the unknown, but it was not as shocking for the individuals concerned as it must be now for those who are displaced by bombs and persecution and who have no idea which country they are going to end up in, or whether they will even be allowed in or will have to remain in refugee camps for years on end, their potential wasting away. The Irish immigrants were delivered safely to their destination in steamer ships not washed up on beaches in makeshift rafts and inflatable dinghies. In 2016 there were estimated to be 65 million displaced people in the world. That is more than two people for every second of the year. This is a subject I will be looking at in more detail later in the book.

The McCourt family was successful at what they did. No great fortune had been accrued by the time I was born, although many fortunes had been made by others in the construction business by then, in a half-century which had seen the rise of many of the modern American city skylines still standing today.

We lived a comfortable lower-middle-class life of the period, a time when most people did not have many possessions but had great aspirations and hopes for what the future might hold materially. The "Great American Dream" was in full flower, and it seemed like there truly was a level playing field when it came to being successful. Everyone could look forward to enjoying a rising standard of living if they worked hard, and that led to a feeling of cohesion and optimism throughout society. Virtually everyone was living better lives than their parents or grandparents had done.

Until I was 10 years old, we were a one-car family, and my mother would stay at home once my father had taken the station wagon to work. Each morning she would position her ironing board in the middle of the kitchen, meticulously pressing the white shirts that we all wore to go to the local Catholic school. Everyone would come down for breakfast at different times and so my mother did not need to lower the bench that was hinged to the wall, which she had to do to accommodate us all at dinner time, as well as adding a card table to the end so there was room for everyone. It was the same routine for every family meal. If there was going to be a more formal event, we would set it up in another room. Once the shirts were ironed, she would line up fourteen slices of bread and spread peanut butter or a piece of baloney on every other piece. She would then finish the sandwiches off and put each one in a brown paper bag with our initials on, sometimes adding a little treat like a Hostess cupcake. Why she bothered to initial them, since they were all identical, I have no idea. Once we got to school, we would then start the business of trading the contents of the bags with other kids.

Each afternoon, when I arrived home from school, having walked back by myself from virtually the first day, Mom would lift me up, put me on the kitchen counter and place my foot onto her thigh in order to change me from my school shoes into my sneakers. She would double knot the laces, give me a pat on the leg and a kiss on the forehead and send me straight back out to play, with the words, "God bless. I love you." Always she finished every conversation the same way. "The last words I will say to any person I love," she explained to me one day, "will always be 'God Bless. I love you.'"

My dad loved to go for drives. Sometimes Mom would make up errands for him at the weekend simply because she knew he was itching to get out of the house and drive around for a bit.

"Do you need anything from the store, Honey?" he'd ask if he was growing bored of watching TV with me. "I need a quart of milk," she'd say, though I know now she usually didn't need anything, because she owned up to me after he'd died, an event which sadly occurred on the day that I became engaged to my future wife. "Come on," he'd say to me, "let's go for a ride."

I would protest because I really just wanted to watch TV, but Mom would nudge me to go with him and in truth it was always interesting because he would never go straight to the store. There would always be something going on in the neighborhood that he wanted to take a look at, like a new house being built, a tree being chopped down, or a dramatic rise in the river levels after a storm. He was actively interested in everything that went on in the world around him and his enthusiasm was infectious.

He was also prone to performing random acts of kindness, a trait which my daughter Alex seems to have inherited. There was a very famous Irish figure in Boston when my father was young, called Mayor Curley. At one stage he was actually in jail when he was elected, that was how popular he was with the Irish Catholic working classes. He ran Boston with an iron fist, and he was a friend of my grandfather's. His personal life was unusually tragic. He outlived his first wife and seven of his nine children and ended up living alone in his old age after leaving office in 1950. When my father was a young man, my grandfather used to tell him that if he had time on the way home from work he should stop by and see "the mayor." My father would stop by Curley's house unannounced for tea, and when my parents got married, the infamous mayor came to the wedding, adding a dash of star quality to the proceedings.

"It was so nice of him to come," my mother would say when she told the story, "but the mayor was so grateful to your father for taking the time to drop by and visit an old man."

It was not unusual for my father to drop in unannounced and chat with someone if he thought they might be lonely and in need of some company, especially older people. I think it's a very Irish habit. As a result, my father never had to call in favors or ask people to do things for him because they would always step forward and volunteer without being asked. He attracted that sort of goodwill simply by being a good guy himself. A remarkable man.

Because Mom didn't have a car until all my older brothers and sisters had grown up, a couple of times a week she and her mother would set out to do all her shopping on public transport because we didn't have a big refrigerator in the house and things had to be fresh. This meant walking a mile up the hill from the trolley stop, weighed down by all the bags. I guess all the walking she did during those years is one of the reasons she is still alive and not walking with a cane at 101 years of age. She always claimed that she had the easier end of the marriage deal since she didn't have to get up at five in the morning to go to work like Dad did, but there was a lot of work involved in looking after a family of nine people: a lot of grass to cut, a lot of snow to shovel and leaves to pick up, not to mention the cooking, washing, and cleaning, and her parents to keep a watchful eye on as they grew older.

Home life was very traditional. Dad would get home at five in the evening, eat his meal, watch the news, go down into the basement to do some job or other, and then go to bed with his evening newspaper and a cigarette. He would be sound asleep by eight thirty. He expected the house to be quiet by then. Phones were still seen as a potential intrusion into the tranquility of home life. If one of our friends rang after that time, he would snatch the receiver up impatiently. "Who the hell's calling in the middle of the night?" he would bark. "Do your parents know you're up in the middle of the night?"

Later we found it funny, but at the time it was embarrassing if you were trying to ask a girl out on a date.

There were none of the scheduled events or activities to get to at the weekends that would be normal by the time I became a parent, like football practice or ballet classes. After lunch every Saturday, Dad would lie down on the couch. "Come on," he would coax me, "take a nap with me."

I would be wide awake and wanting to do things, but my mother would shoo me over to please him, and I would curl up with my head on his chest and his arm around my shoulders. He would be asleep in a minute and Mom would see that I was wide awake, bright-eyed and eager to do something else. She would gently lift his arm off me so that I could escape without waking him.

A lot of political capital is made of the climate of fear that has been engendered this century by international terrorism, but we lived under a constant threat before the concept of terrorism ever came to the shores of the United States. As well as having many of America's biggest industrial companies in Watertown, we also had the Boston Arsenal there, which meant that during the Cold War, the authorities, for whom the unprovoked attack on Pearl Harbor was still a relatively recent memory, were always worried we would be a target for communist bombs. Every day at noon they would test the air-raid horn and every Friday we had to practice the drill of diving for cover under our school desks. We all had to have our names written inside our ties so that we could be identified if we were killed in an attack, but none of us ever really thought anything of it.

Dad was a man who made things happen, using his own hands if necessary. He built a little cabin on a lake up in New Hampshire, and each year he would have a project to improve it, like putting new electric in or insulation or building a deck. It made me realize that if you wanted something you could always find a way to make it happen. In those days, a working-class family didn't hire other people to do practical jobs like that; we did them ourselves. There was no hot water until much later, and every Sunday morning that we were there Mom would boil a kettle so we could wash up in preparation for going to church. If you were slow to get up and the others got ahead of you, the water would be a good deal less clear and a good deal less warm, teaching us the advantages of acting fast and decisively.

There were two bedrooms in the cabin, one for the girls and one for the boys, and Mom and Dad would sleep on a pullout couch in the living room, which was pretty noble of them now that I think about it. At the end of the evenings they would watch the news because my mother liked to see the weather, which always came at the end. Dad would then get up to brush his teeth and would send us all to the bedrooms with the words, "Time for you guys to get out of here."

They wouldn't turn the TV off immediately, so I would be able to hear the theme tune for *The Tonight Show* with Johnny Carson, which ran for thirty years, and then I would listen to his opening monologue from bed before they switched off to go to sleep.

As a teenager I had all the usual jobs, like a paper route, cutting grass in the summer, and shoveling snow in the winter. When we were at the cabin,

I would work the gas pump on the lake, which was a great job for a young boy because all the girls would come across the water at the weekends in their bikinis to fill up their dads' boats. I was already learning that work could be fun as well as profitable. Once I was old enough, I would work every day of the summer vacations. I would work on a construction project with my father Monday to Friday and at the boathouse on the weekends. Occasionally I would work for an electrician as well. It was just taken for granted that we would all work as soon as we could. At the end of each term, we would come home from school or college on the Thursday, maybe take the first weekend off, and then start our jobs on the Monday, working all the way through till we went back to school. We all had jobs while we were in college, too. I don't remember there ever even being a conversation about it, it was just what all the kids we knew did. The work ethic was built-in from the start.

My siblings and I all ended up following very different paths in life once we left home. One sister married a dentist and helped him out in his practice; while another became a professor, author, and the first female dean at Loyola University of Chicago; and the third became a successful independent management consultant and married a judge. One brother became a contractor and proudly continued the family tradition, another a lawyer and managing partner of the Boston office of a national law firm, and the third, Frank, became a successful real-estate developer; so successful in fact that he ended up buying the Los Angeles Dodgers baseball team off Rupert Murdoch, which made him very wealthy when he eventually sold them. He became pretty high profile in the media and now owns Olympique de Marseille football club, the only French soccer team to have won the Champions League, beating AC Milan in 1993.

Frank and I are opposites, but in many ways just the same. We often partner up in business together even though we approach challenges in very different ways. He tends to start at the top and drills down, whereas I tend to start at the grassroots of problems and work upwards, but we nearly always end up at the same point.

One of the subjects we talk a lot about is the need for charities that help young people to identify and achieve their dreams. We are both in agreement that one of the most annoying things about charities is that they so often feel obliged to describe themselves as being "not for profit," rather than talking about the things that they are for. It seems to us to be a very negative approach. As in politics and business, it is always more inspiring to be "for" something rather than "against" something.

When he's talking about our family history, Frank likes to mention that our grandfather was one of the early owners of the Boston Braves, who are now the Atlanta Braves. Our grandfather actually used to play cards with five other guys and one of them, a construction guy called Lou Perini, was rich and had bought the Boston Braves for a couple of thousand dollars. He told the others that if they wanted to throw in a few bucks they could be partners with him. I think they each threw in fifty bucks including our grandfather.

My mother had been my grandfather's secretary, which was how she met my father, when he came home in the summers to work, and later in his uniform from officers' training school. She had been offered two jobs, one with John Hancock Insurance for $15 a week and one with the John McCourt Company, who she had never heard of, for $16 a week. If John Hancock had offered another dollar a week, I, and all my siblings, wouldn't exist. She likes to tell people that the other girls in the office would warn her to stay away from Dad because he was "trouble," but he wasn't easily put off. He was crazily in love with her by then and would pretend that he had papers which needed typing and would ask my mother to do it for him, making sure he stopped by her house later to pick them up and spend time courting her. Their love for each other stayed just as strong to the day that he died. It was a remarkable love affair.

One of her jobs each afternoon was to take the money down to the bookies to place bets for my grandfather. She would have had no experience of that world from her own father, who never gambled or drank.

I don't remember either of my parents ever asking any of us what our plans were for the future; they just assumed we would sort things out for ourselves. But whatever it was they did to rear us, they did a great job. There was never any patience with whining in the house. If the girls were monopolizing the bathroom and I went to my mother to complain, she would simply shrug and point outside. Her philosophy on life was that if things went wrong you should do your best to fix them, not whine, put one foot in front of the other and keep moving forward, and know that whatever problems you have, someone else has much worse.

"Just remember," she still says, "it is all about attitude, gratitude, and acceptance."

For her hundredth birthday we celebrated with a centennial tour, one stop being at my house in Ireland. There we gave her an oil painting by Peter Tunney that my brother organized. It combines the two words "gratitude" and "attitude." She stood at the end of the meal (at this point, in true McCourt fashion, it was well past midnight), to give a speech of thanks to us all and repeated yet again her belief in accepting whatever life throws at you and feeling gratitude for whatever you have.

It was a lesson other people I admired would reinforce later in my life. There is never any point in whining about the past, or "crying over spilt milk"; you simply have to get on with life and sort things out for yourself. I quickly worked out that if things have gone wrong then you just have to change them and continue to move forward again. That was probably the most important lesson I ever learned. I was once in a buffet line at a private J.P. Morgan event next to Rupert Murdoch, after he had sold the Dodgers baseball team to my brother, Frank. The team had been doing better since he sold them, and I casually asked if he now regretted getting rid of them. He looked at me with an expression of complete incomprehension, like I was weird for even asking such a thing. I turned to Jimmy Lee, vice-chairman of J.P. Morgan, and asked him why I had just received such a death stare.

"You asked him a question about the past, about a decision he has moved on from and which he can do nothing about," Jimmy explained. "It's irrelevant to him, and so his brain doesn't know how to process it."

There is such an important lesson to be learned there, exactly the same one that my parents had taught us as children. So many people go through life claiming that something that happened to them years before is the reason that they have not been as successful as they would have liked. But setbacks happen to everyone and you can always start again. If you have one goal and you fail to attain it for whatever reason, you simply need to forget about it and create some new goals.

Many years later a CNBC camera crew followed me all over the world for two weeks in order to make a documentary for a series about entrepreneurs. When they interviewed my mother, they asked her what my "secret sauce" was. Apparently, she told them that it was the fact that I had always been able to talk to anyone, whether they were 3 years old or 80 years old, and that they would feel like I could relate to them. I don't know if that's true, but if it is, then that would explain a lot about what has happened to me, and the opportunities I seem to have stumbled across right from the start of my career.

When I was still quite young, I happened to meet the world-famous photographer Richard Avedon during a photo shoot he was doing with some senior executives. He must have fired off a shot of me because a few weeks later I received a beautifully packaged print of the portrait with a letter from Avedon saying, "I met you a few weeks ago, and you were the only one who treated me with respect, as an equal, so I want to give you this as a gift." At that stage he was charging around $50,000 to do portraits for people.

I went to see him to thank him and he asked me if I liked the picture.

"To be honest," I said, "I don't think I look that great."

"Believe me, son," he said, putting his arm around my shoulders, "one day you will look back at that picture and you will think you look just great." He was so right.

As Dale Carnegie famously said: "You can make more friends in two months by becoming interested in other people than you can in two years by trying to get other people interested in you."

My father died when I was thirty-two years old, so I have grown used to my mother being someone who lives on her own. Every year since my father died, I bring her to stay with us in St. Croix in the same little cottage. If she sits for more than a few minutes on the porch, trying to read the newspaper, all sorts of people will stop by to talk to her because she is just such a pleasant person to spend time with. In my whole life I have never heard her say an unpleasant word about anything or anyone. It is very obvious why Dad was so much in love with her.

She is 101 years old now, and I still take her away each year to the same efficiency apartment on the beach that she used to go to with my father. There are some people in the world who suck the energy out of you, while others imbue you with energy, and they are the people that you want to spend time with. My mother is an energy giver. If anyone taught me how to be an entrepreneur it was her and my father, not any fancy entrepreneurial course.

- If you want to be a creative entrepreneur, apply the same lessons to every aspect of your life and go out looking for the knowledge you need.
- You do not need to go to college or read a textbook to find it.
- Never complain about anything; just fix the problem yourself.
- Be interested in other people and learn to talk to everyone.
- Accept whatever comes along and be grateful for everything you have.

6

Work on Your Strengths, Forget Your Weaknesses

"If you had two like him, you could march into hell and put the fire out."
—Jim Monroe (on Drew Dix, the first enlisted Special Forces soldier to receive the Medal of Honor)

"I began a revolution with 82 men. If I had to do it again, I would do it with ten or fifteen and absolute faith. It does not matter how small you are if you have faith and a plan of action."

—Fidel Castro

Because I achieved good grades in high school I was allowed to get out into the world and look for a work project halfway through my senior year. I chose to work at the Watertown Massachusetts Police Department. Going out with the detectives was an exciting experience and I decided, at the age of 16, that I wanted to become a cop. This was despite the fact that I had already been accepted to a couple of colleges: St. Anselm in New Hampshire, where I knew I would be able to play ice hockey, and Georgetown University in Washington, DC, which was more highly rated academically. To be honest, I was a little ambivalent about college because all the men I knew in our area were contractors, cops, or firemen. It was just what everyone did.

53

"I've applied to be a cop instead of going to college," I told my father one evening when he arrived home from work. "They've told me I'm going to make the training program."

To my surprise he was totally relaxed about it and, as usual, totally supportive. "If I was you, I think I would consider going to college first and then becoming a cop later. It would be better to be a smart cop," was all he said, leaving the final decision completely up to me.

Luckily the decision was then taken away from me when the job offer was withdrawn because they said they had minority set-asides to meet and I wasn't part of any minority group. In my youthful indignation it seemed totally unfair to me and I complained about it at length at the family dinner table a few days later, breaking the family rule about not whining.

"Listen," my dad interrupted, "you're bitching to the wrong guy. You need to talk to your congressman."

"Who's my congressman?" "Tip O'Neill."

Tip O'Neill was a highly controversial politician. He would later go on to be one of the longest-ever-serving Speakers of the House of Representatives. He was already known as a vociferous opponent to US involvement in the Vietnam War and was the most prominent Democrat to call for the impeachment of President Nixon after the Watergate scandal.

"Where's his office?" I asked.

"He has a little office in Watertown Square," Mom said. The next day I made my way to the tiny local office and found a man called John Carver sitting behind the desk. I introduced myself and told him my complaint about being rejected by the police for not being part of any minority group.

"So, you play ice hockey, huh?" he said, gesturing to the logo on my sweatshirt.

"I was captain of my team," I said excitedly. "Where do you play?" he asked.

"B.C. High," I said. "Where did you play?" He replied with just one word: "Harvard."

That was impressive news for any 16-year-old hockey player. It was my antics on the ice that had earned me the nickname "Goose," because I had a habit of winding up the opposition by "goosing" them from behind with my stick. I wasn't the most talented of players, but I worked harder than everyone else, which is pretty much how I see my whole life. I was probably the worst of the good players but the best of the average ones, and I made up the difference by working my butt off. I've never regretted the fact that I was not born with any great star talent in anything. I actually think that possessing a great talent can sometimes lead people to being less well-rounded individuals, simply because they concentrate on the thing which is their talent too early to the exclusion of trying everything else. At the same time I do think people should be encouraged to play to their individual strengths, if they have them.

The paradox here is that when you are young everybody tells you to "work on your weaknesses," but those weaknesses, almost by definition, can only be improved by a small, incremental amount, while you can improve upon your natural strengths almost infinitely if you go about it the right way. You can easily see the results of that sort of single-mindedness in all the top sports where kids are taken off and trained relentlessly to compete in one particular event, whether it is baseball, football, or tennis.

The same is true at the highest levels of the academic and artistic worlds. Great violinists and pianists spend all their time practicing with their instruments; great scientists spend all their time in laboratories and comparing notes with other scientists. In his book *Outliers*, Malcolm Gladwell examines the factors that lead to outstanding success and talks a great deal about the "10,000-Hour Rule." Based on a study by Swedish psychologist Anders Ericsson, Gladwell explains that it takes at least that long to become "great" at any expertise, whether that is playing a guitar or programming computers. In fact, I think 10,000 hours probably only gets you as far as being a highly proficient professional in most things, and it requires a great many years of dedication to become great.

Gallup has done a lot of research into the costs to society of not developing people's strengths when it comes to making management appointments, and the figures are shocking. They estimate that only about 1 in 10 people possess a natural talent to be able to manage other people and that organizations appoint the wrong people to management posts about 80 percent of the time, which not only leads to business inefficiencies but to social problems as well, with people leaving jobs because they are being badly managed. I suggest you read *First Break All the Rules*, a book from Gallup, and then do the "Strengths Finder" tests at the end.

I believe the problem stems from the way we channel the talents and enthusiasm of children. By encouraging them to spend time working on their weaknesses, parents and teachers are trying to make them more like everybody else, when they should be encouraging them to develop the talents that make them different, make them special, and make them stand out from the crowd. It is often the special people who end up making a difference to the world and all of us have something that makes us special if we are encouraged to search for and develop it.

I remember sitting on the steps at home on the day when Mom broke the news to me that I was going to have to repeat second grade. I was a little young for the grade, but I was also a slow reader. I was deeply disappointed, but she always made that sort of bad news much better. No one was kinder or more understanding and supportive. All through university and the first few years of my business career, I would call her the night before an important test or meeting, just to get her good wishes.

According to educationalist, writer, and inspirational TED speaker Sir Ken Robinson, "We are living in times of revolution. I mean this literally, not figuratively. Humanity now faces challenges that are unprecedented in our history."

He goes on to explain that we need to think differently about ourselves, starting with education: "Education often promotes a narrow view of ability, as do many corporate organizations. As a result, many people are unaware of the variety of their talents and depth of their potential.

"Every country on Earth at the moment is reforming public education."

The first reason for this, he explains, is economic, because we all want to work out how to help our children find their places in the future economies, even though we can't predict what those economies will look like. At the same time, we are trying to give our children a sense of cultural identity while still being part of globalization.

"The trouble is," he says, "they are trying to meet that future problem by continuing to do what they did in the past. . .a system which was conceived in the intellectual culture of the Enlightenment and the economic circumstances of the Industrial Revolution."

One of his conclusions is that the increase in the diagnosis of ADHD in children is largely a result of the children being bored at school because of inappropriate teaching during a time which is the most intellectually stimulating in history. Instead of "putting them to sleep" with drugs, we should be waking them up. This is a First World problem. No one is drugging the kids in Africa or India, which is why they will be thinking more creatively and will eventually replace the old-fashioned, slow-thinking countries of the currently prosperous but conventionally educated West if things don't change. The very existence of the bottom third of American universities is now under threat.

Virtually all school curricula in America are geared around helping children to get good results in standardized tests. Those tests help them get into colleges and business schools. There they do more standardized tests in order to get to graduate school. If they do really well, they get into Harvard where the whole premise of the business degree is to teach them to think "outside the box" – the exact opposite to everything they have been taught up until then.

In their haste to make everyone behave to a perceived "norm," many parents, particularly in the more affluent areas of America, seek medical answers to behavioral differences in the form of drugs like Ritalin. Although there are obviously cases where medicine offers answers to children with real problems, all too often kids who simply function "differently," particularly the ones coming from more aspirational communities, are given drugs in order to suppress their natural personalities and make them think and act the same as everyone else; to make them, in other words, "less odd."

No one, however, suggests that you should do anything to change the way the sports jocks think or act, even though they may be very low performers in the classroom, because they have a visible talent that the entire school can see on the playing field, whereas a kid with the same amount of talent who is making music in the basement will be looked at differently.

To a degree, things changed with the rise to world prominence of the technology geeks. Once all the richest people in the world were seen to be coming out of the computing and technology businesses it was no longer so uncool to be one of the techy kids at school. But it is still considered uncool to have the sort of short attention span that leads to the labeling of kids as ADHD and to the medical professions drugging them in order to narrow their field of attention. It would be infinitely better to look for subjects that will hold their attention in the first place and which they will then excel at. If they have trouble concentrating in the math class let them go to the English class, and vice versa. Many of the answers to the problems of the future are potentially locked away inside the heads of these unique kids, so we must be very careful not to throw away the keys due to our hunger for conformity and our fear of the unfamiliar and unusual. We need divergent thinkers more than ever, and we must take care not to destroy their uniqueness through standardized education. As our educational curriculum becomes more and more set in concrete, we are becoming more like the giant corporations that end up being strangled by bureaucracy and are over-taken by the smaller, fleeter, more creative companies.

Maybe a kid who is acting up in the classroom, or letting the team down on the sports field, should be in the music school or the art room or creating software for online games in the computer room. Maybe he or she is just on the wrong track and if they tried something else, they would end up being the next Albert Einstein or Angela Merkel, the next Bob Dylan, Martin Luther King, or Beyoncé.

Geeks are only left alone in childhood if they have some outstanding tal-ent that is traditionally acceptable, like playing a musical instrument, because then they are labeled "gifted" instead of "special needs." Sometimes they nev-ertheless can't tell jokes and may be socially awkward, but nobody thinks this is a problem anymore because their "genius" will be their ticket through life. If they play the piano to concert-level standard, then their teachers and their parents are more likely to overlook the fact that they are unable to kick a ball and have trouble socializing with kids their own age. If they have not yet shown any special talent everyone is going to be worrying and trying to make them more "socially acceptable." If a guy is captain of the school football team, however, no one is going to worry about the fact that he is at the bottom of every class or can't concentrate for long enough to pass an exam. No one will ever label him "special needs." Likewise, if a girl is beautiful and popular, and a cheerleader for the school team, no one is going to overly worry if her exam results are disappointing. People have preconceived notions of "talent," and many young boys and girls who may have them are overlooked.

The social pressures to conform to some idealized stereotype have always existed, but it is no longer appropriate because it is the outliers, the people who think differently, the ones who used to spend all their time reading books and now spend it staring at screens, who will most often be able to see how the models can be blown up and how things can be changed for the better. They are the people who will be questioning the status quo at every level and solving the problems the world is now facing. The conformists have tried doing things their way, and it no longer works, at least only for a small percentage of the world's population. If we are going to find ways to lift the bottom five billion out of poverty, then we are going to have to look outside the traditional boxes and come up with different ideas to everything that has gone before, and that process must start in the classrooms of our schools.

Even those of us who are unable to think originally ourselves need to be able to accept that other people do think differently and embrace those differences, particularly if they are thoughts around regulatory change, consumer behavioral change, and technological change. The outliers have historically been significant players in many of the major revolutions in thought (no one would ever have mistaken Einstein for a great athlete), but that is usually despite the discouragement they faced along the way, not because they were encouraged to look for new ways of doing things. Imagine how much more they would have been able to contribute if they had been nurtured and encouraged to come up with unusual – perhaps even unthinkable – ideas throughout their education.

There is also a strong case to be made for cross-fertilizing different disciplines in order to come up with something new. At the University of Southern California, I recently helped in a small way to invent a class called "M(2e)," as in "Media, Economics, and Entrepreneurship." The university had a problem in that their journalism school students weren't getting jobs after graduating. I suggested to Dean Wilson of the Annenberg School for Communication and Journalism at USC that we teach them a little bit about not being afraid of numbers, so that they would be better equipped to work for start-ups. Dean Ernie Wilson brought me in as their inaugural Economist in Residence to stress test the idea after Professors Chris Smith and Gabriel Kahn rethought the whole concept of how you teach journalism. Professor Chris Smith had read my opinion pieces in the *Wall Street Journal* and had been using them as supplementary teaching materials in his class. I'm also the inaugural Executive in Residence for Entrepreneurial Economics and Innovation at Georgetown University.

The problem seemed to be that the students all wanted to work for the famous, prestigious corporate names and were not numerate enough to understand that these companies had only a limited lifespan ahead of them. They needed to be able to understand how the new business models were going to work so they could either start their own businesses or work for smaller, more flexible online companies. Simply to be self-employed, which most of them inevitably will be for most of their working lives, they needed to understand basic finance, a subject that had been largely ignored in their journalism training in the past.

Those among the older generations who have been in charge of society for the last century, including the teachers and police, have all spent too much time talking *at* the more unconventional members of the younger generation rather than listening *to* them. If cops listened to the thoughts and ideas of kids from culturally isolated neighborhoods now and again, maybe those kids would listen back and a real dialogue could be opened up about how to close the gap between the two sides, which in some cities seems to be as wide today as it was 30 years ago. If teachers listened to the pupils, they generally considered to be too time-consuming and too individual, those children would be able to help the teachers see more clearly into the future so that they would be more able to work out ways to make it better for everyone. If the education system encouraged people to be original rather than to compete to be the best of the same, they would uncover a much broader spectrum of ideas and answers to the big questions and problems that society is wrestling with.

The older generations complain that the kids today don't know how to communicate with one another because they are always on their phones. But they are on their phones having conversations and collaborating. They are doing it all the time, far more than any generation before them. The older generations are also under the impression that they don't read or write any more, but that is actually what they are doing all day long through texts and messages. They are using the written word more than any generation at any time in history. There has never been a generation with so much potential for collaboration.

By the same token, if Republicans and Democrats, capitalists and socialists would actually listen to one another they might find common ground and be able to work together for the good of all the people they represent. Our whole society is set on "transmit" and "compete" all the time, seldom on "receive" or "cooperate."

None of these thoughts, however, had yet occurred to the teenage me as I sat in Tip O'Neill's local office that day, after losing my place on the police training scheme because of minority set-asides. John Carver and I talked casually for a while about hockey and I complained a bit more about the unfairness of my situation.

"Do you really want to be a cop right now?" he asked eventually, much as my father had done. "Why don't you go to Georgetown? You can always become a cop when you come back. Or maybe you'd rather be in the FBI or something else."

As he talked, he took out a piece of paper, wrote a note, slid it into an envelope and sealed it. "Why don't you go and enroll for Georgetown and while you're in Washington take this to Tip's office and give it to a woman named Dolores Snow?"

Since I couldn't now get onto the police training course anyway, I went to Georgetown as he suggested. On the first day, I enrolled in my courses and then took the bus to Capitol Hill, found Tip O'Neill's office, and asked for Dolores Snow, who was his administrative assistant. When she came out, I gave her the envelope and watched as she opened it in front of me and read the note inside. Carefully refolding it she gave me a quizzical look.

"When do you want to start?" she asked. "Start what?" I replied.

"John Carver says you're going to be working here as an intern. Do you have your class schedule?"

In those days, with no smartphones or laptops, it was normal to carry around something like that in your pocket so you knew where you should be and at what time. So I pulled out the schedule of my classes and gave it to her, and she told me when I should turn up to work.

From that series of accidents, I ended up working for Tip O'Neill, one of the biggest characters in Washington, and I received a paycheck at the end of the month, which was so unexpectedly large for someone working a few hours here and there between classes I thought it must be a mistake. My older brother, Terry, was working full-time on Capitol Hill by that stage, for a Republican Senator, Paul Laxalt, who was a very close friend of Ronald Reagan. I told him what I'd been paid.

"Holy shit," he replied, "that's the same as my pay. No wonder the government is in such a financial mess."

When I queried the amount, Dolores assured me it was no mistake; it was the minimum government pay.

I would often be in the office on Saturdays, and as it was a quiet day I would get to talk to the Speaker. Tip would sometimes come back from the White House and talk about how he and Reagan didn't see eye to eye on things but how they would still manage to reach some agreement. Tip would always say, "I'd rather have 50 percent of something I want, than none of something I want." It seems like that attitude is lost in politics today. No one seems to want to take half and let the other guy have half – (what in the business world would be known as a "win-win" situation) – they all want to take it all.

With politicians like Tip, it was all about listening and compromising. Now, it's all about fighting, being seen to be hardline and all-or-nothing, sometimes even going as far as shutting down the government and causing gridlock. Listening and compromising are critical skills in business and should be seen in the same way in every other walk of life. It seems now that governments create more problems than they actually solve by forgetting this fundamental truth and always looking for opportunities to set up gladiatorial contests between the two sides and between individuals. The old way of governing had a lot of similarity with business. The new way of governing has no similarities with running a successful business; it has more in common with the pop TV culture of confrontation and competition, with everything being about winners and losers rather than collaboration. This is the stimulus for my documentary series *What if. . .?*, which is about artists from different backgrounds collaborating and cooperating on a similar theme as opposed to competing, and which I will be talking about in more detail later in the book.

Tip had a great deal of style. One Saturday I came into his office and found him sitting with his feet up on the desk, smoking a cigar. I assumed he had come in to read some legislation in preparation for Monday's vote.

"Mr. Speaker," I said, "can I do anything for you?" "Nah," he said picking up the TV remote. "Millie has some girls over at the house, and I just thought I would watch some golf."

Another time he came back into the office after having breakfast with Reagan in the White House. "That man," he grumbled, "does not know how to serve breakfast. A little glass of orange juice, a doughnut and a cup of coffee. . .," he shook his head sadly. "That man does not know how to serve breakfast," he repeated. "At least we could have had some bacon and eggs, huh?"

In the Speaker's office the water cooler was one of those upturned glass bottles that always weighed a ton. You don't see them anymore. We used to call them "bubblers" on account of the noise they made. Tip had the water flavored with cranberry juice because cranberries were one of the main crops of the New England area. I thought that was a nice personal touch, and I think of it whenever I see cranberry juice.

Since I was studying sociology, I also worked as a probation officer's aide in Anacostia, a low-income neighborhood of Washington. I was beginning to learn where my future strengths might lie.

My first adult entrepreneurial adventure was running keg parties at Georgetown. I quickly worked out that if I allowed girls in for free it would lure in more boys, and I could then raise the ticket price for them. It was a huge hit, and others copied the idea and used it for thirty years at Georgetown, until they eventually outlawed rolling a keg into your dorm hall.

My mother wrote me a letter the first month I went away to college, telling me that she'd been into my room to pick up my dirty socks and realized it was going to be the last time she would be doing that as a daily task. The last of her seven children had grown up and she wouldn't be seeing another pair of dirty socks on the floor until we came home for Thanksgiving. Next thing I heard she had got herself a job at the local mall, which was a shock to me because, like most self-absorbed kids, I had never imagined her existing outside the house and family. I called home from the college payphone to find out what was wrong.

"Why are you working, Mom? Has Dad lost his job?"

"I just wanted something to do," she laughed, "everything is fine."

So, if things had gone differently, I would have been a cop, like so many other young men I knew. Congressman Joe Moakley used to say the same thing every time he saw me.

"Oh, Dave," he would chuckle, "I feel so bad for you. You missed your dream by less than an inch – you should be out there now, walking the beat in the cold rain and being shot at!"

Moakley would tell another story too. "I remember going to Tip O'Neill's office to see the Speaker," he would say. "Dave was coming out of the office as I went in. Once he'd gone, Tip took the cigar out of his mouth and said 'Joe, that kid's gonna go somewhere.'"

I have no idea whether that story was true or not, as I had left the room, but I liked it when he told it anyway.

- Be brutally honest with yourself about what your strengths are, then look for ways to develop them.
- Never be afraid to speak up if you want something.
- Never be afraid to introduce yourself if you want to meet someone.
- Always look for ways in which you can work with those who disagree with you. A compromise is always better than no deal at all.

7 | Being Interested in Everything

"You can waste your life drawing lines. Or you can live your life crossing them."
—*Shonda Rhimes*

"Being a good listener is absolutely critical to being a good leader."
—*Richard Branson*

"We keep moving forward, opening new doors, and doing new things, because we're curious and curiosity keeps leading us down new paths."
—*Walt Disney*

Because I was the youngest child in the family, I often got to go places with my parents because there was no one else still at home to look after me, all my older siblings having gone off to make their own ways in life. I didn't mind being the last one at home because I liked to be with the grown-ups, listening in on their conversations, learning about adult life before I actually had to go out into it. Everything I saw or heard interested me.

Working in Tip's office as an intern provided the same rich and far-reaching education and information for a young man who wanted to understand how the world worked and how he might be able to succeed himself. It expanded the circle of my knowledge and opened up new horizons to me. Part of my job in his office was to read all the mail that came in and fill in a chart enumerating the main issues that people were complaining or worrying about, listing the geographical areas they were writing from and the number of letters we were receiving on each subject. I was soaking up everything that came across my desk and talking to everyone who passed within my orbit, making contacts that would prove invaluable in the years to come. Back in those days, by the way, 90 percent of our politicians' contributions came from his or her district. So, although money can be poisonous, at least the money, the votes, and the power were all in the same district. Today, a politician in one part of the country, might get 90 percent of their campaign contributions from an area outside of the area they represent, which is wrong.

After I had finished at college, I joined Dad and one of my older brothers, Rich, in my dad's construction business. Dad was by then on the verge of retiring but kept working for a few more years in order to give us time to settle in and learn the ropes. In order to do that, he'd had to buy out a cousin and had cashed in his life savings, which were all in Polaroid stock because a friend of his had worked for the company. My brother Rich was actually away skiing when our father demanded to know if he wanted to go into the business or not. My brother agreed to do it, but I didn't need a call, I had always wanted to be in the family business and couldn't wait to get started. Today, the original family construction business is proudly run by my three very capable nephews.

I was immediately looking around for ways to move the company into new, more interesting sectors. It was around 1980 that I read an article in *Time* magazine about cable television not being able to reach into the more densely populated urban areas because the laying of the cables under streets and sidewalks was just too disruptive and expensive. The article started me thinking.

The arrival of cable television was a big story at the time, just as providing everyone with faster broadband is a big story today. In 1972, Chuck Dolan and Gerald Levin of Sterling Manhattan Cable had launched the nation's first pay-TV network, Home Box Office (HBO), which was also the first premium programming service in the cable television industry. The first program distributed on the channel, the 1971 film *Sometimes a Great Notion*, starring Paul Newman and Henry Fonda, was transmitted to 325 Service Electric subscribers in Wilkes-Barre, a city in Pennsylvania I would come to know well. In 1973 they sold HBO to Time Life, by which time it only had 8,000 subscribers across 14 cable systems, all of which were located in Pennsylvania, and it was suffering from a significant subscriber churn rate. By 1975, however, HBO had around 100,000 subscribers in Pennsylvania and New York State and had begun to turn a small profit. This had led to the creation of a national satellite distribution system that changed the business and caused an explosive growth of program networks.

The next service to use the satellite was Ted Turner's local television station in Atlanta, broadcasting mainly sports and movies. It was distributed by satellite to cable systems nationwide, and became known as the first "superstation," WTBS. By 1980, almost 16 million households had become cable subscribers, and in the same year Ted Turner also founded CNN (Cable News Network), the first television channel to provide twenty-four-hour news coverage and the first all-news television channel in the United States. (In 1991, Ted would become world famous when he married Jane Fonda, the actress known for her campaigning and left-wing politics as well as her many starring roles in Hollywood, her two Oscars, and the fact that she was Henry Fonda's daughter.)

Even in 1980 I had a strong feeling that telecommunications in general was going to be the industry of the future, even though at that stage we had not yet seen the birth of mobile phones in any form that we would recognize today. Even cordless landline phones were a novelty. The only serious innovation that had happened in the phone industry in the previous hundred years, apart from the expansion of the color range for handsets beyond the original black, had been the invention of press-button dialing. Because AT&T (American Telephone and Telegraph Company) had a monopoly on the industry, they had no need to be any more innovative than that: people still had to buy from them because there was nowhere else to go.

In 2017, however, American consumers alone, according to Deloitte, looked at their mobile devices more than nine billion times a day – that one statistic demonstrates just how totally the telecoms revolution has changed the way we think and behave.

In the television industry things were moving a little faster in the early 1980s, but still nothing like the speed of the developments that were to come in the twenty-first century. The digital industries such as technology, communications, and media, which I went on to spend my life in, have grown in productivity four times faster than the physical industries which had existed before. They also outpaced physical industries in every other way, including job growth and revenue growth. Digital industries have, by definition, more tech employees and a higher tech spend (physical industries still produce 70 percent of output but only 30 percent of IT spend), but if we increased tech spend in physical industries, they too would be transformed and many of them would not need to be blown up for fear of being run over by creative new industries.

There are examples today of physical industries that have been transformed, such as shale oil in the energy business and e-commerce in the retail sector, but by this stage technology should have totally revolutionized every single industry. But most physical industries are slowed down by being heavily regulated, which means they are expensive to operate in and consequently tend to resist any sort of potentially costly experimentation. The digital economy, however, has been relatively free to invest and innovate wherever it sees fit, which has led to the creation of spectacular and inexpensive products and services, many of which would not have been deemed possible fifty years ago. Traditional physical industries that haven't yet been revolutionized will all be overthrown if they do not act quickly.

The telecoms industry is still far from peaking. In 2017 Deloitte reported that: "the telecom sector continues to be a critical force for growth, innovation, and disruption across multiple industries."

We have come a very long way in a very short time. At the beginning of the 1980s, cable was only being used to get a signal to suburbs where there was bad reception on traditional aerials, so that they could receive the main over-air TV stations. Ninety percent of the time, therefore, the cables were being carried above ground via poles, in order to cause minimal disruption during construction. You could not, however, stick poles up in city centers; you had to dig up the streets and sidewalks – which caused a great deal of disruption.

One of the greatest advantages of listening to other people talk about their work and their industries is the opportunities that arise for the cross-fertilization of ideas. Over dinner one night Dad told me a story about how they had paved a runway at Logan Airport and the FAA had then made a new rule, saying that they had to install a line of special blinking landing lights all the way down the center.

"So now we have to rip up a brand-new runway," he grumbled. "The old system of lights has been fine ever since the war. I don't see why they have to add these new ones. But it could be worse; the engineer at the airport tells me they have this rock saw which will cut a slit in the middle of the runway which we can insert the wire into without digging up the whole thing."

"Why can't we do the same thing with cable TV?" I suggested.

It was like a light going on in my head and was probably the first time I experienced the birth of an idea which had the potential to "blow up the model" and as a result completely rethink the cost structure of an industry. In addition to making a slit in the road I had the idea of extruding the conduit with the cable already inside and rolling it up in a big reel, a concept that I then branded.

Not that I hadn't had ideas before. I was constantly brimming with them. Sometimes opportunities to come up with radical solutions to problems come about simply by being in the right place at the right time and being willing to volunteer your services, even if you are unsure whether you can actually do the job. I was at Logan Airport on the evening of 23 January 1982, when a World Airways DC 10 went off the end of the runway as it came in to land, crashing into the harbor and getting its undercarriage stuck in the mud, with the tidal waters lapping up to the wings. Two people, Walter and Leo Metcalf, who were sitting in the front of the plane went into the water and were never seen again, which became a great mystery since there was only about four feet of muddy water at the time and no strong currents, but everyone else survived.

In the following days, the airport reclamation teams were having real difficulty getting the plane out of the water because every time they cleared around the landing gear the tide would return and bring the mud back in. I had an idea that I thought might work, so I told the prime contractor I could do it.

When there is an apparently intractable problem, people are nearly always happy to hand the responsibility over to anyone who is confident enough to volunteer to find a solution and confidence was something I was never short of.

Confidence, by the way, is undoubtedly a necessary part of being successful, but it is also vital that you have around you a group of people who are willing and permitted to voice their opposition to your ideas. If you don't listen to people who have different perspectives on problems from yours, your self-confidence is likely to lead you to making a lot of misjudgments. Confidence without capability is one of the deadly sins. People will help you with your lack of capabilities but not if you are arrogant about it.

I started by simply building a dyke to encircle the plane. Once the dyke was there, we pumped the water out and the area around the crash site stayed dry long enough for us to attach ropes to the plane and pull it back onto dry land.

I got a real buzz out of finding solutions to problems which no one else had seen, but I really wanted to find ideas that would give me a route into the telecommunications industry before it started to take off in the way I thought it might. I had a feeling that the laying of cables might be my opportunity.

- Never be afraid to step up and volunteer for a job if it offers a real learning opportunity.
- Always look for ways that technical advances in one industry can be applied in another.

8

Getting Taken Seriously

"When the whole world is silent even one voice becomes powerful."
—*Malala Yousafzai*

Just about everyone has a bright idea from time to time for an invention that they are sure will make them a fortune. You hear the theories being expounded all the time if you spend enough evenings hanging around in bars (not a pastime I would recommend to anyone who actually wants to get something achieved), but very few people are then able to take that idea and make it a reality, particularly if it is potentially disruptive and will meet with resistance from the established industry that it is likely to disrupt. Any creative entrepreneur who wants to achieve anything concrete needs to be able to execute their ideas effectively or, more often, to find someone to work with who is skilled in execution.

When you are young and inexperienced it is hard to convince older, "wiser" heads that they should invest in your untried and revolutionary ideas until you have a track record of success – but how do you achieve that track record if no one will buy into your ideas?

It's all too easy for a rich and powerful industry to crush an individual who puts forward an idea which they believe might endanger their revenue stream and their profits in the short term, particularly if that industry operates as a monopoly or near-monopoly. If entrepreneurs want to turn their ideas into reality they have to prove to potential investors and potential employers that they can be taken seriously and that they can add value. They have to convince naturally cautious people that they will be able to execute the ideas they are selling.

I was still convinced that the cable TV business had opportunities that would fit with our construction experience. I needed, however, an opportunity to get a foothold in the cable industry. I could see that there was potential for enormous growth, even though I did not yet understand the full potential of all the future technologies that those cables would end up carrying. At that stage few people had even an inkling of the data revolution which was about to change the way we did virtually everything; in the early eighties just sending television pictures down a cable was a futuristic enough concept for most people.

I knew that there were bids going in to install the first underground cable television network in Boston and everyone was saying that Time Warner was bound to win the contract. I decided they were the people I needed to reach out to if I wanted to get the job of laying the cables. Anyone I talked to, however, about putting in a bid, told me that there was no point since our company had never done any cable TV work in the past. It was undoubtedly true that we had no track record of working in the cable industry, nor had we worked for Time Warner in any other capacity, but everyone has to start somewhere, right?

There was a lot of controversy in the media about the installation of the network because many people were worried about how much it would cost and how much disruption it would cause to their lives during the installation process. The more I read about the disruptive potential of the industry, however, the more I thought we should be part of it.

Every couple of weeks I would go back in to Time Warner's offices and ask to get on the bidders' list for doing some work and each time I would leave empty handed. Then one week they told me they had a problem in the northern suburbs of Boston, where heavy rains had flooded the manholes that their cables ran through and made it impossible for them to service their networks.

"Do you have any pumps?" they asked. "Do you know anything about pumping out manholes?"

"Yeah, of course," I assured them, "we can pump out those manholes for you in no time."

I then rented a pump from Logan Rentals in East Boston with my best friend from school, Jim Finnegan, (who later married my personal assistant and still sends my mother a poinsettia every Christmas), and we went around the streets doing the job ourselves. It wasn't hard, and it meant that now we could actually say we had done work for Time Warner, so that when they "inevitably" won the contract we would stand a better chance of being able to get onto the bidders' list.

I felt very pleased with myself, until it was announced that Cablevision had beaten Time Warner to win the contract. I had backed the wrong horse. All the effort I'd put into winning over the people at Time Warner had been wasted, and I had to start again, trying to get a foothold in a completely different company and convince them that I was the man for the job.

I quickly called a friend who still worked at Tip O'Neill's office, Kevin Peterson, and asked how I could get onto Cablevision's list of approved contractors. He put me in touch with a guy who used to be Cablevision's lawyer, who responded to my pleas and wrote to Chuck Dolan, the billionaire pioneer who had founded Cablevision after selling HBO, asking if I could be given an opportunity to bid. Permission was granted. We had a chance.

Chuck was one of the few people in the business who could see that cable could be about more than simply improving reception for consumers. He believed that the creation of cable networks would make it possible to make available all sorts of things that were not available on the broadcast channels such as movie channels, public interest programs, educational material, and pay-per-view events.

Jim and I then put together a bid, at which point we realized we didn't even know what "CATV" stood for, having assumed it just meant Cable TV. When we went off to research it (in those pre-internet days you still had to physically go places to find things out), we discovered it stood for Community Antenna Television. Having straightened all that out we took our bid in to an engineer named Jerry Cruzan at Cablevision's office at 21 Merchant Row, Downtown Boston.

As we were leaving, I noticed that there was a bar directly opposite, so I stationed my girlfriend there and asked her to make a note of all the other

bidders she saw going in and coming out, so we had an idea who the competition was likely to be. Because of helping out my dad over the years, I knew
most of the players in the construction business who would be likely to go for
this sort of work. The way she described them at the end of the day, I knew
exactly who each one was. When she told me about the guy who turned up
in the cleanest pickup truck she ever saw, I knew it was M. Dematteo Construction. If she described a big African-American guy with a broad, friendly
smile, I knew she meant a good friend of mine named Danny Fernandez.

Danny was a big character. I was having breakfast one day with him at
a place called Charlie's and I noticed he hadn't taken his baseball cap off.

"Take your hat off, Danny," I said. "We're having breakfast here, and you
look like an asshole."

"I can't," he grunted.

"What do you mean, you can't?"

"I had a hair transplant, and the doctor fucked me."

"What do you mean the doctor fucked you?"

"He gave me white man's hair!"

He lifted his cap and I could see that the clump of transplanted plugs in
his previously bald dome had indeed grown out dead straight. I'm afraid it
was one of the funniest sights I had ever seen.

Once I had worked out who the opposition were I then went back to reinforce my pitch and made sure I mentioned all the rival bidders that I guessed
had been in, dropping in a little piece of extra information about each one that
might make them seem less attractive as potential suppliers, while at the same
time reinforcing the idea that I really knew my industry inside out.

"When can you start?" Jerry Cruzan asked as one of his standard questions. It was then October.

"We're ready to go any time," I replied, as casually as I could manage.

"Really?" He was obviously surprised. "You could do the work during
the winter?"

"Of course we can," I said, wondering why he was so startled by this news.

"All the other contractors have told us that you can't get permits in
Boston during the winter except for emergency construction."

During the winter Boston's already narrow streets become even more
constricted, with the snow piled up on one side and all the cars being
forced to park on the other during the busy holiday shopping period.

The authorities did not want anyone digging up the already crowded streets unnecessarily and causing further congestion. There was also a problem with the steel plates that we would use to cover the trenches at night, which would then be pulled up by the snowplows as they cleared the streets of any new snowfalls.

So I had committed us to delivering something which those in the know had said could not be done. That either made me sound like a genius or an idiot. I could not afford for it to be the latter. Sometimes naivety gives you the confidence and that confidence gives you a chance.

By sheer luck I had learned from another Cablevision employee that they were really keen to get the system going by the end of the year so that they could start signing up new customers in the New Year. Talking to someone else I discovered that because Chuck had been unable to persuade the banks to lend him money for such a speculative venture, he had raised the money by offering limited partnerships, which were able to take advantage of special tax write-offs. Investors in the project would however only be able to benefit from tax losses on the development costs in the current year if they hit that deadline for being operational. In order to satisfy the tax authorities that they were "operational," they had to be able to sign up customers by the New Year, which was why there was such a sense of urgency in order to meet their commitments to their investors. I didn't fully understand the details, but it seemed likely to me that these people had only invested in order to be able to get these tax advantages. If that was the case, then Cablevision had backed itself into a corner and would be bound to choose the only contractor who had promised to do the job during the winter.

The next time I went in to Cablevision, I asked if this was the situation and Jerry confirmed it was. "In that case," I said, "I can guarantee you will be up and running by January first."

"In that case," Jerry replied, "we'll give you Phase One of the work."

- Always gather as much information as possible about the job and about all those involved in it. Do your research.
- Preparation, preparation, preparation.
- Never be afraid.
- Let fear be your tailwind, not your headwind.

9 | Achieving the Impossible

"I'm interested in things that change the world or that affect the future and wondrous, new technology, where you see it and you're like 'Wow, how did that even happen? How is that possible?'"

—*Elon Musk*

"Knowing what must be done does away with fear."

—*Rosa Parks*

I'd got the job, but only by promising to do something that more experienced contractors than me had deemed to be impossible. How was I going to deliver on my promise if I couldn't get a permit to dig up the roads?

To make matters even worse, Phase One, it turned out, was scheduled to happen in Chinatown, an area made up of huge, tightly packed old buildings and narrow streets. It would be impossible to dig them up without causing major disruption, even in the height of summer, but virtually impossible if everything was covered in ice and snow. There was no way I would be able to deliver on my promise in that area. I had to find a way

77

to persuade Cablevision to start in another part of the city. I explained my problem to a friend who worked in the mayor's office.

"Why does Chuck want to build there first?" he asked. "Because it's closest to the Head End, where the signals all come in."

"Well, the mayor is getting the hell kicked out of him in East Boston because they're building a new runway at Logan International and the planes are coming in really low over the houses. If we told him you were going to wire East Boston first, giving the locals better television reception, that would give him some good news to tell them. He would be happy to give permission for the construction to go ahead if it gave him some good news. I'm pretty sure he would be willing to deem it an 'emergency.'"

At that moment a light bulb came on in my head. East Boston was connected to the city by a tunnel, which would mean that we could just run the conduit right under it without having to dig up any streets and without having to worry about snow or whatever other adverse weather conditions might be raging up above. This could be my way out of the tight corner I'd talked myself into. There was also a section of elevated expressway leading to the tunnel, under which I could pin the conduit on the way to the tunnel for the rest of its journey to East Boston.

So I went back to Cablevision and told Jerry Cruzan that I happened to know that the legendary mayor, Kevin White, would really appreciate it if we could take the cables out to East Boston first, instead of Chinatown. He was happy to do the mayor a favor, and as long as we got at least one part of the network up and running by the end of the year, he didn't care which part it was. He gave me the go-ahead.

Because we didn't have to dig up any major roads, a job that would have taken months if I had tried to do it in Chinatown took no more than a few weeks. Not that it was all plain sailing. I was, after all, still a rookie at this job and it was inevitable that I would make at least one major mistake. What I hadn't appreciated was that the cables being used at the time were so rigid it was impossible to pull them through the conduit. By the time I installed the conduit, it was full of right angles and there was no way we were going to be able to pull the cable through them. The only solution was to cut the right angles out of the conduit and let the cable snake on its own from one piece to the next. Because it was sheltered beneath the expressway and the tunnel, we could do that, although it didn't look particularly neat. For years afterward

I'd be driving back to Boston to visit my parents and I'd see that cable hanging loosely between the elegantly placed conduits and would laugh to myself.

It was meant to be an emergency measure, to make sure we didn't miss our deadline, but the cable stayed the same for twenty years, until eventually they pulled down the expressway and ran the road underground in what was known in New England as "The Big Dig" (a multibillion-dollar project which created fifteen years of construction work and jobs, the last gift to Boston from Tip O'Neill, who pushed it through Congress before he retired).

Now, however, I could rightfully claim that we were "experienced" in laying a cable system.

- Never assume anything is impossible.
- If you have a problem, visualize the ideal solution and then work backward to see how that can be achieved.
- Start young. All your life you are in a war with time. If you don't act quickly time will win every battle.

10 | Tell Your Story to the World

"If you can't explain it simply, you don't understand it well enough."

—Albert Einstein

Happy with the way we had delivered on our promise, Cablevision gave us the contract for Phase Two of the project, and soon after we got started, I was having my weekly lunch with my brother Frank in the same restaurant, in the same booth, halfway between our two offices.

Frank and I are the same person and at the same time exact opposites. I'm obviously better looking (in reality we look like twins). We see problems the same way but attack them from opposite ends. Where I attack them with marketing, he attacks them with math. Many of my good ideas came from him and many of his came from me, although we both "claim" that the other's ideas suck.

"Have you any idea how big a deal this cable installation you are doing is?" he asked. "You should really try to get the whole contract off them now and you should also hire a public relations company to tell the entire world that you are constructing the most difficult cable system in the world."

His advice set off another light bulb in my head, and I started asking around about public relations people who might be able to help. At that stage, all my time and attention had gone to selling the company's services for specific projects and then to overseeing the project management itself. I hadn't given any thought to the wider subject of marketing and building a reputation for myself and the company, both inside and beyond the industry. Now that I was taking the time to think about it, I could see the sense in spreading the word about what we were doing so that next time I went knocking on a potential client's door, they would at least have heard about us. I realized, however, that I needed the help of a professional.

My investigations led me to a guy named Frank Kerr, a retired reporter who could have been sent for the job from central casting. He had everything, from the big beer belly and tie at half-mast to the coffee stains down the front of his shirt. He would have a cup of coffee in his hand all morning and a bottle of beer all afternoon, but he seemed to know exactly what he was talking about.

Frank agreed to write stories for me and quickly showed that he was a genius at spotting angles and setting up photo opportunities. We ended up with hundreds of front-page stories about the "construction of the most difficult cable system in the world." He had an immaculate reporter's eye for a story, commissioning photographers to create great artwork of me pulling cable under the tunnel or mounting equipment on top of high buildings with spectacular views. He was also brilliant at creating news angles to make stories attractive to editors, like moving the diggers to the other side of the street one day in order to make it look like we were putting cables under Paul Revere's house, teaming the picture with a headline that played on Revere's famous line "the British are coming!"

In every encounter with the media he kept repeating the line, "Dave McCourt is building the most difficult cable network ever," and once a few magazines had printed that, he would simply quote them as being the originators of the quote rather than himself, and so the story would roll and grow like a snowball. It's a technique I still use today, always including the words "The *Economist* described him as having 'impeccable credentials as a telecom revolutionary'" in every relevant piece of corporate literature or press release, and also the quote from the journalist who described me as "Che Guevara in a suit," which I always liked.

Frank taught me that if you are trying to sell people a story, they need to be able to grasp what you are talking about in one clear, crisp sentence. It's like the famous "elevator pitch" in Hollywood. If you can't sell a producer a story in the time it takes — anything from thirty seconds to two minutes — to reach his floor in the elevator, then you are never going to get your picture made. At the same time, Frank Kerr taught me that if he made the editors' lives as easy as possible by writing the articles for them, and if the articles were written to a high enough standard to go straight into the magazines, that is what would happen. If the photographs were also of a higher standard than the magazine's staff photographers could manage, they would end up being printed, too, sometimes even on the front covers. Being featured on the front covers of respected trade magazines has an incredible effect on a person's credibility in the industry concerned.

Back at street level, the problem with the cable being too rigid to go around corners seemed to be a major stumbling block for future contracts, and I knew we had to think of a radical way around it. The cable industry had evolved incrementally out of telecoms technology and I knew I had to find a method of doing things that would be a tailor-made solution to this particular problem. I could imagine the end result I wanted to achieve and needed to work backward from there to find a path to achieving it — the archetypal inventor's approach.

Why, I wondered, did we not take the cable to the factories that were making the conduits for us, and simply ask them to manufacture the conduits with the cables already inside so they could be rolled in 100-foot reels rather than 10-foot lengths? That way we would be able to lay the cables in one stage instead of two, radically cutting the construction costs, and we would also have overcome all the difficulties of trying to thread the rigid cables through the conduits once they were in place. Jerry Cruzan was incredibly supportive of the idea, and I would never have got it off the ground without his help. So many times in my career I have only succeeded in bringing my ideas to fruition because of the support of someone who had the power to help me execute the plan and make it real.

The guys at the factories said they could do it, and so at a stroke we had found a way to lower the cost of laying cable systems by as much as 80 percent at the same time as solving our initial problem of how to go more easily around corners. We had "blown up the model" of cable laying and created a solution that was made to measure for the burgeoning cable television business.

We had cut construction costs by 80 percent! Now we had a story that Frank Kerr could really get his teeth into. Now we truly were the most innovative cable television contractor in the country, and soon we would grow to be the biggest as well, working in all the major cities in America and heading abroad to set up networks all over the world.

- If you can't tell your own story, no one will be able to tell it for you.
- Find a supporter and then nurture them.
- If you have a story to tell, tell it succinctly, illustrate it beautifully, and tell it over and over again.

11

Radical Ways of Getting Paid

"Life shrinks or expands in proportion to one's courage."

—Anais Nin

I had become a modern nomad, moving to each city while the job was under way, which made me the first male in the McCourt family to move out of the Boston area since my grandfather first arrived from Ireland.

Business was brilliant, but it was volatile too, and then Chuck Dolan at Cablevision refused to pay me for the Boston job, claiming they had run out of money for the project. It was not a new story in the construction business. The contractors are always the ones who developers let down first in these situations, because once the thing is built, they don't need us again. That makes life tough for any contractors who do not have capital to fall back on and who are existing on their cash flow, as I was. If you are running a company with high wage bills, one client holding up a payment can make the difference between staying in business and going under.

It doesn't matter how brilliant your business idea is, or how effective you are in executing it, or how much good publicity you get in the media –

if you don't get paid at the end of the day, the whole business model turns to dust. This was a big enough debt for it to look as though I would go broke unless I acted fast to cut my costs. So I was forced to lay everyone off, which hurts when you have assembled a really good team, because you know they will go off and work for other people and will then be unavailable once you are back on your feet and start hiring again. I also sold my equipment, even my pick-up truck, while I worked out what to do next.

As usual, I talked to as many people as I could in my search for a solution. In fact, I was going on about it all the time because the problem kept going around and around in my head. I was in the Sevens Bar on Charles Street in Boston's historic Beacon Hill area with Tip O'Neill's son, Tommy, and Donny Chiofaro, a highly successful property guy and a former Harvard football player. I was complaining again about Chuck Dolan refusing to pay me. Donny, growing tired of listening to me, grabbed my tie, hauled me across the table toward him and bit my nose.

"If somebody bothers you," he said, "that is what you do."

"What the fuck?" I protested.

"We're trying to have a beer here," he said, "and you just keep on bitching. Either do something about it or shut the fuck up!"

It was a wakeup call. He was right; I needed to do something. This was a grownup version of my parents' intolerance of whining children, with added cussing and biting, and I got the message. Donny now denies he bit my nose, but you don't misremember a moment like that, at least I don't.

So I needed to do something about the situation. I had a friend who had recently had a wall of glass bricks put up around the shower room in his fashionable loft apartment. He had been slow to pay the mason and had told me a story about how the mason had showed up at his door with a large hammer.

"I'm here for one of two things," the mason told him, "either you give me a check or I'm taking my work back."

"What did you do?" I asked.

"I wrote him a check," my friend said, shrugging like the answer was obvious.

The story stayed in my head, as I realized the pursuit of a legal battle could be fruitless, so it occurred to me that I could use the same sort of leverage if I threatened to dig up the cables that I had laid for Cablevision.

I checked out the idea with my brilliant but volatile Greek attorney, Nick Kensington, who had been introduced to me by my brother Frank.

"Would I go to jail if I dug up a bit of the cable to make my point?" I asked.

"I don't think you would go to jail for something like that," Nick told me, so I decided to give it a go.

Jim Finnegan and I took a digger out and did exactly that. We only had to take up a small piece of the cable to shut down the whole system. Dolan, who is a mild-mannered, quietly spoken Irishman, had a hatchet man who was a fiery Italian called John Totta. John went ballistic, screaming abuse at me down the line, ranting about the "Irish Mafia," using some words I hadn't heard used outside a locker room and some I'd never heard before anywhere, before slamming down the phone.

"I think he's upset," I told Nick, who instantly panicked and denied that he had ever told me it was okay to take such drastic action.

Cablevision tried to intimidate me at meetings by bringing in big-time lawyers, ex-prosecutors, and retired FBI guys, insisting that the cables were now their property, not mine, but I held out, saying that until they paid the bill the cables belonged to me and I was going to be taking them back. Nick Kensington, who attended the meetings with me, became so angry and frustrated at one stage that he banged on the table so hard that he stabbed himself with his own pencil, driving the lead deep into the palm of his hand. Within a couple of days, however, Cablevision had capitulated, and I was paid everything I was owed.

Jim Crowe, a close friend and great telecom revolutionary, used to refer to Nick as "Nick the Prick," and once described him to me as the "best lawyer in America to hire, as long as you're wrong."

There is an image of Bostonians, especially if you have a thick local accent as I do ("an unreconstructed Boston accent," as one journalist put it, or "his thick, working-class Boston accent," as the BBC phrased it), that we are all just one degree of separation away from Whitey Bulger, the Irish Mafia boss who was played by Johnny Depp in the movie *Black Mass*, was the inspiration behind Jack Nicholson's performance in *The Departed*, and who was top of the "Most Wanted" list in America for years. Whitey was a big hero in the area, for all the wrong reasons, at the time I was going to school, and his story created an image that stuck to all of us who lived in the same district. He was generous to those who lived locally, but he was also known to be a murderer. As kids, after hockey or football practice, we would go to what we called the "Dirty John" sub shop, on the border of the Old Colony housing projects, which was owned by Whitey, and we would often see members of his gang just hanging around.

The connection with Whitey became more personal when I later built the first competitive phone company in America. I had this idea that we could cut our construction costs by partnering with power companies so that they would let us use their poles quickly and for free. I did the first deal with a power company that was then called Boston Edison. The head of security at Boston Edison at that stage was John Connolly, a former FBI agent who was later convicted of racketeering, obstruction of justice, and murder charges stemming from his relationship with Whitey Bulger. (In *The Departed* he was played by Matt Damon and in *Black Mass* by Joel Edgerton.)

John's downfall came about when the Department of Justice decided they wanted to shut down the Mafia, because they had seen how successful Rudy Giuliani had been as Mayor of New York with his "zero tolerance" approach and they wanted to do the same nationwide. John was told he could make a deal with Whitey Bulger and the Irish Mafia in South Boston if Whitey would agree to give them evidence on the Italian Mafia in the north of the city, which was run by the Angiulo brothers. I happened to know the Angiulos because Mike, the son, was co-captain of the local hockey team with me.

As a result of the deal everyone was told to keep their hands off Bulger as long as he steered clear of the drugs trade and there were no murders. So John turned a blind eye to everything, but it emerged later that he was being paid by Bulger and then he was caught tipping Bulger off when the FBI were coming for him. As a result of John tipping him off, Whitey went on the run and was only caught 12 years later, in California at the age of 81.

The story goes that the FBI lured him down to the underground garage below his apartment block, where they ambushed him and ordered him to get down on his knees. Whitey allegedly told them to "fuck you with the kneeling down" because he had clean white pants on. He later blamed his arrest on the fact that he had lost his attention to detail in his retirement. If he had still been in business as a gangster, he would have known better than to go down to a basement just because someone asked him to. Instead he would have gone out the back door and been 50 miles away while they were still waiting in the dark for him. I guess gangsters are like any other kind of business person: if you get lazy and lose your attention to detail you start making bad decisions. Anyway, John Connolly was working for Boston Edison before he was indicted, and we became friends. He used to come over and take the kids out fishing and on trips around the FBI. My son, David, still has an FBI sweatshirt that John gave him and wears it sometimes when he's watching football.

It was stories like these that made people think that everyone in Boston was "connected" in some way to the Mafia. I was doing a deal with a guy one time and his lawyer slid a note across the table to him. Because I had spent so much time as a contractor, I had learned to read upside down from looking at other people's quotes when the client had laid them out on the table opposite me. So I could see clearly what he had written.

"Be careful, he's from South Boston."

It's not a problem for people to think that you might be tough, because it can help in negotiations. The Boston accent can also be a little disarming because the Harvard and Princeton guys assume you're stupid while the scrappy entrepreneurial guys assume you're tough – and of course growing up the girls thought you were a "bad boy," which was seldom a bad thing.

When the BBC wrote a profile of me for their News website the journalist wrote, "If you ever saw the fifty-eight-year-old drinking in an Irish bar in his native 'Southie,' the blue collar part of the US City, you'd be minded not to annoy him."

When Cablevision eventually paid up, I found myself in a strong position. Since I had laid my workforce off while I sorted things out, I had no big wage bill and the money went straight into the bank and stayed there, which is an unusual position to be in, in the contracting business. I now had a breathing space to think what I should do next.

- If the bills don't get paid you don't have a business.
- Business is like chess: you need to see your leverage points two moves in advance.
- There comes a point in every business person's career when they have to be tough.

12

Taking Risks and Grasping Opportunities

"Twenty years from now you will be more disappointed by the things that you didn't do than by the ones you did do. . .Explore. Dream. Discover."
—*Mark Twain*

"Normal is not something to aspire to, it's something to get away from."
—*Jodie Foster*

Going to the London School of Economics (LSE) during my junior year abroad at Georgetown, and traveling so far from Boston, was a big adventure for me. I had chosen to go to a British university because at least I knew I could speak the language. I arrived in January 1978, missing one of the biggest blizzards in recent American history. When I got there, I discovered that the LSE allowed for independent thinking to a degree that I hadn't encountered at school. Although a lot of American universities claim to support independent thinking, when it comes to exam time, you need to be sure your independent thought is the same as your professor's if you hope to get an A grade.

I learned a lot in the year I was there, sharing a flat at 220 Cromwell Road in Earls Court, a bohemian part of West London at the time, popular with Australian travelers and the less well-off Arab visitors who were just starting to arrive in London in the seventies. My flatmates were actors studying at places like the Royal Academy of Dramatic Art and the famous London Academy of Music and Dramatic Art, which was just across the road. One of them was Paul Provenza who went on to make a big name for himself in comedy, starring in the TV series *Northern Exposure* and directing the film *The Aristocrats*, which was at one time the number-one-selling direct-to-home DVD in America. There was an exotic beauty named Wendy who I dated, and the other guy, Kevin, appeared in *Les Misé-rables*. He had a beautiful voice, and I spotted him many years later when my wife took me to see the show on Broadway on our first Christmas together and went backstage afterward. We went on to dinner with him at a Chinese restaurant; it was someone's birthday and the whole cast of the show was there, singing "happy birthday" to him, a fabulous sound.

I saw Bob Dylan playing just down the road at the Earls Court stadium and the first McDonald's in London opened up in Earls Court Road while I was there – a big event for an 18-year-old. The college where I took some classes was on the King's Road in Chelsea, which was then the center for the emerging punk-rock movement. They were strange, exciting times for a young guy from Watertown, Massachusetts.

I hitchhiked from London to the bottom of Italy then talked myself onto a boat going across the Mediterranean to Spain for free. I discovered an entrepreneur called Freddie Laker had started a cut-price airline, and I was able to cash in the return ticket that my parents had bought me and buy a cheaper one on Laker Airways. By the time I got on the plane home I had just two dollars left in my pocket, not realizing that they were going to charge for food (one of the ways Laker kept ticket prices so low, and a first in the industry). The lady sitting next to me took pity and very kindly bought me lunch and someone else let me share their taxi as far as Harvard Square in Boston, which got me halfway home at least.

Ten years earlier, another student, Maurice Bishop, had returned from the LSE to his homeland, the Caribbean island of Grenada, and headed up the local Marxist party, which was known as the New Jewel Movement. He took over the island in a popular revolution in 1979 and made himself prime minister of the "People's Revolutionary Government."

He was known to be working closely with the communist Cuban government, which was helping him to build a new airport with a runway that seemed, to the ever-vigilant American intelligence sources, to be long enough to take the sort of Soviet military planes that carry heavy equipment like tanks and missile launchers.

Despite his popularity and his Marxist doctrine, Bishop refused to hold democratic elections and stifled the free press and any opposition politicians who dared to criticize him or the New Jewel Movement. There were rumors of people being arrested and tortured for their political views and a climate of fear was building on the island.

Dissatisfaction with Bishop swelled and in 1983 there was a counter-revolution which culminated in him being marched by a mob to the top of a hill and tied up with his pregnant girlfriend, who was also minister of education, and several other members of his cabinet. They were then executed by firing squad and there were also rumors that the bodies were chopped into pieces, set on fire and that the remains were thrown into the ocean. Nothing is certain about the event except that no one has been able to locate the bodies since, allowing the myths to grow.

Just knowing that such a fate for a formerly popular leader was even feasible should have been a warning sign for me about the political temperature of the island.

When I left Georgetown at the beginning of the eighties, many of my friends were still working in Washington; one of them, Mike Castine, was working in the Reagan White House. One day, during the period when it looked like Cablevision was not going to pay me and I was going to go out of business, I was having lunch with Mike. He was explaining to me how 70 percent of US imports and exports sailed through the Caribbean on the way to us and that the president was concerned that there was a lot of communist influence creeping into the poorer islands. The Cubans and the Russians were spending huge amounts of money educating and influencing the Caribbean leaders and President Reagan was worried that they were going to build a whole string of Cuba-style enclaves just off the coast of Florida. Grenada was currently top of this list of worries.

"The president's theory," Mike explained, "is that if there is no unemployment in the islands, communism won't seem such an attractive option to them. So we need to put money into those economies to help them create jobs."

After the coup and the murder of Bishop and his close colleagues, the whole population was then put under curfew. It seemed a potentially danger-ous situation, and there was a medical school on the island with a bunch of American students. Rescuing the students gave President Reagan the excuse he needed to send in the Marines and kick out any Russians or Cubans who could be found on the island in order to "liberate" the people from communism.

The story of this invasion was all over the American newspapers and one of the details that I noticed was that the runway at the airport was described as being "only half finished." Since I was supposed to be a con-struction expert, I thought it would be worth buying a ticket to Grenada to see if I could bid for the job of finishing it.

I was still a naïve kid of 28 and when I got there, I found the job had already gone to one of the big government contractors, but I made it my business to find out everything that was going on around the island in my usual energetic manner. A *Boston Globe* report of the time described me in an article: "It was difficult for anyone to miss him. . .he was every-where. . .he was absolutely all over the map."

Among others, I managed to befriend Herbert Blaize, who was the interim prime minister of the island, and the same newspaper report describes me as answering most of the questions on the prime minister's behalf at a press conference held to talk about the democratic elections that then had to happen. I think I just wanted to help him get elected, and the natural enthusiasm I always have for the causes I take up must have showed through. Herbert was an old, quiet guy, who walked with a cane and talked so slowly he never seemed to get to the answer quick enough, so I wasn't able to stop myself from jumping in whenever a journalist asked a question – I was simply too young to know any better. "I'll answer that if I may, prime minister. . ."

Looking back now I can't believe I had the nerve to do that or that eve-ryone around him allowed me to get away with it, but I think it illustrates the importance of youthful thinking and enthusiasm in creative entrepre-neurs. When you are young your risk profile is very different because you have less experience of all the things that can go wrong, and less to lose if they do. Today, I might be embarrassed to arrive in a strange country and just introduce myself to the prime minister, but then I thought nothing of it.

Looking back through the files now I seem to have crammed a great deal of frenetic activity into that period. In 1984 I was voted "Boston's

Outstanding Young Leader" and appeared in a book called *Boston's Most Eligible Bachelors* along with such varied figures as John Kerry, future presidential candidate and secretary of state during Obama's second term, and Paul Corsetti, a journalist who went to jail rather than reveal his source before a grand jury investigating a murder. The book was published by the *Boston Herald*.

If you want to do something really creative, it is a good idea to start when you are young, because the one thing everyone is bound to run out of sooner or later is time. The sooner you start the race, the further you are likely to be able to get. There is also the question of energy levels. I know a lot of great business people who decide at some stage to take a break and slow down, intending to come back to their careers later. They seldom return and never manage to pick up the speeds they were previously capable of. People might wonder why some of the elderly business creators, like Rupert Murdoch, continue working for so long once they have achieved all the wealth and power they could possibly need. The answer is generally that they simply love what they do, and they know that if they started to slow down, they would no longer be able to perform at the levels they find stimulating.

I find that now, in my early sixties, I am acting more like I did when I was 25 than when I was 45. In the middle of my career I was employing 20,000 people. I had a company jet and a yacht and all the other trappings of success that are expected in the corporate world, and they were using up a great deal of my energy. Owning a yacht sounds like a wonderful luxury but actually it is a chore and leaves you less time to be creative and to actually get things done. Now my kids are grown up and I have shed many of these trappings. My risk profile has become more like it was when I was just starting out, leaving me with much more energy to think creatively and continue taking big gambles.

Herbert Blaize and I were standing together one day, looking out over the ocean. "You see those fishermen?" he said, pointing at the boats bobbing on the waves below. "They all make the same mistake. They buy a new engine and then they hire the cheapest man they can find to run the boat and eventually their engine breaks down. If you're going to invest in a new engine, get yourself a qualified man to run your boat."

He wasn't the most eloquent man, but his point was that having the money is only part of the equation; you need good people too. In business terms he was saying that you need to allocate both financial and human capital to any project if you want it to be successful. To me those fishing boats seemed symbolic of how other aspects of life in Grenada were being run. Interested outside parties were investing in capital equipment and facilities, but there wasn't the skilled manpower available to run and maintain them once they were built.

When the two of us were chatting about ways to reach the people and convince them to vote for him in the election, which he was now obliged to hold, Herbert pointed out that it was hard to talk to the people directly because Grenada had no television station.

"So, why don't I build you a television station?" I suggested. In my youthful naiveté it didn't seem to me that it would be that hard a thing to do. "Then we could put on a political show so that you can get your views across to everyone."

"Okay," he grinned, "you do that."

An engineer called Mike Adams was working for us part time while studying for a PhD at MIT, which was enough to lead me to assume he was smart. I asked him to come down to the island to build the TV station with me.

"I can't," he said, "I'm writing my thesis and anyway I promised my wife I would take her on vacation. . ."

"Come on," I coaxed, "just bring her to Grenada; she'll love it."

Grenada is one of the loveliest of the Caribbean islands, although at that time there were still Marines stationed around the place and coils of barbed wire on the beach, which made his poor wife a bit too nervous to stay for long, but Mike became as enthused about the project as me and stayed on.

We had been living in quite a nice hotel in the beginning, but we soon ran out of money and had to move to a cheaper one, where many of the rooms didn't even have doors. Later we discovered that the Russians had used the building to billet their soldiers while they were constructing the runway. Mike was woken one night by a young woman walking into his room and asking if she could use the bathroom. Taken aback, and half asleep, he agreed, and she emerged back into the room a few minutes later, stark naked. Mike assured me the next day that he had insisted she leave, and of all the people I was working with he's one of the few I would believe would actually be able to resist temptation on that scale. From then on, we started calling the place "Hotel California."

I had a driver who only had one arm and used that to drink while he drove his rackety, stick-shift car. He'd step on the clutch, shift gear, take a sip of his beer and then take hold of the wheel again to bring us back onto the right side of the road. For some reason it all seemed okay to me, maybe because I was young or just because that was the sort of thing that happened on small Caribbean islands. He taught me a lot of new expressions.

"He's just a gone-ass," he said of one of my engineers.

"What's a gone-ass?" I asked.

"You know," he grinned and took another swig of beer, "a guy who is so old his ass has gone and can't keep his pants up anymore."

So from then on, anyone who was old was "just a gone-ass." "Do you think there's going to be another revolution here?" I asked one day.

"Oh no," he shook his head, "we're good here for at least six months."

"Why do you think that?"

"It's the rainy season," he shrugged, as if it was the most obvious thing in the world that no revolutionary would want to get wet.

I informed the prime minister that we needed a piece of land on a hill where we could put a tower to transmit the signal around the island. He gave us a map that marked out all the abandoned government buildings to see if any of those would be useful. Mike by then had done his research and found a location on a high hill which he thought would be ideal, but I had spotted the old Cuban embassy, which had stood empty ever since the Cubans had been kicked out. It was the perfect building for all our needs, including housing for whoever came to work at the station, although it wasn't on a hill. When the prime minister asked which piece of land we wanted, Mike was pointing to the top of the hill, and I was grabbing his hand and guiding it over the map to the abandoned embassy.

The prime minister gave us the building, and Mike was just going to have to figure out how to get a signal out to the rest of the island; if anyone could do it, he could. He had a huge brain and great processing power, and he soon learned as much as anyone with all the qualifications. Our next problem was where to find employees to set up and run the station. That was my job. Mike could solve any problem that was possible – he left the impossible to me.

"Why don't I go to Boston University?" I suggested. "It has a broadcasting program. I'll tell the administrators that we'll offer a junior year abroad to any students who would like to take it up. We don't know anything about setting up a TV station but these kids do."

I duly went to the university, made my pitch and they kicked me straight back out again. So I went to one university after another, gradually working my way across from the East Coast, being turned down every time until I reached Central Missouri State University, right in the middle of America, where I had never been before and where they completely understood and accepted the deal that I was offering. I pitched the idea to a guy called John, who had the scent of booze on his breath.

"Ah," he said as I finished my pitch, "you want to create a TV station just like Edward R. Murrow would want it to be!"

I said, "Exactly!" (And then later I looked up Edward R. Murrow. Ed Murrow was a famous broadcast journalist who made his reputation during the Second World War and went on to pioneer television news. He played a big part in bringing down Joe McCarthy and ending the communist witch hunt in the fifties.)

"Then I'm in!"

From then on, my elevator pitch became "this is TV like Edward R. Murrow would have wanted it," making it sound like the great broadcaster was my uncle or something.

"Oh, by the way," I said, remembering what the prime minister had said about the importance of having trained people to run things once you have built them, "we are going to be sending Grenadians to you so you can give them free tuition and put them up in your dorms in the same way we will be putting your students up in our dorms."

They agreed to take 14 Grenadians every semester, which was probably more Grenadian kids than had ever had a university education on the island, which got me treated like a bit of a national hero for a while.

Once I had been in Grenada for a while, I realized I had overestimated the number of television sets there were on the island. Since there was no point broadcasting if no one could watch, I went to Sony and persuaded them to donate a load of sets, which I took around to the village bars. These bars were generally no more that lean-tos on the sides of the road where someone would be roasting corn and chicken and selling beer and whiskey to the local guys, who would hang out there through the evenings and often during the days as well. Most of Grenada is like a rainforest, the villages shrouded in a triple canopy of trees, and before long you couldn't drive anywhere at night without seeing the eerie blue glow of a television screen reflecting off the dark trees above.

By being so high profile in such a politically volatile location, I must also have been taking some big political risks, although I was too young to realize it at the time. Pretty soon, the TV station was reaching all the 110,000 citizens of Grenada, when the biggest newspaper only reached 5,000. That made me the biggest media owner on the island, with 95 percent of the people getting their news only from me. That sort of monopoly is bound to make you a potential target, and this was a country where they had just murdered their ex-leader and his cronies, and where my station manager, Larry Upton, a former Boston TV sports announcer, felt it necessary to carry a pistol in his trunk at all times.

The students traveling to America, of course, were allocated well-appointed dorms whereas the ones coming to Grenada were packed into one room with no running water. In the mornings they would have to walk down to the ocean and wash there, but none of them complained since Grenada is about as close to a paradise island as you can get. I think in the four years we ran the scheme, only one kid ever went home early to his mother. It was a dream job for anyone wanting to become a broadcast journalist because they got to write stories, edit them, and then go on air with them. It was a great experience and it was also great for the prime minister to have a way of communicating with his people and for the islanders to have their own station.

On one occasion, Walter Cronkite, the man who personified television journalism in the United States (he was known as "the most trusted man in America"), and who had retired a few years earlier from his job as anchorman on CBS news, landed on the island in his sail boat and came up to the station to see the kids. On another occasion, President Reagan flew in and made a speech in which he joked about hoping to sell some of his old movies to the station, while our reporter filmed him for that day's news.

I tried to buy some content for the station, but it was all way too expensive, so I decided we would make our own. We did a cooking show, a talk show, a kids' show – anything that we thought the locals would enjoy. We would also broadcast political shows so the prime minister could get his messages across. I had to explain to him that he couldn't go on alone in the run-up to the election, that he had to allow the opposition equal time, bearing in mind what had happened to Maurice Bishop when he tried to silence the opposition during his time in power, but still, the programs helped Herbert to get fairly elected. Sometimes I think someone on my staff would let him see the questions the day before so that he could sound a little smarter and more eloquent in front of the camera, a practice which would not work today (Hillary Clinton got into a lot of trouble during her presidential campaign when it came out that someone had showed her the questions in advance).

Once the programs were on tape, I would then try to sell them to other islands. I would transport them by bicycling down to the airport and asking someone who was flying out to take the tape and deliver it to a certain address, at which point they would be given 10 dollars. The recipient would then go back to the airport and do the same thing to the next island, so that the tape would eventually make its way all the way up to the top of the Caribbean. The other stations would then pay us for the content, although sometimes they wouldn't get around to it and we would have to go collect the money in person. We called them "the bicycle tapes."

Catching the planes was always a bit hit and miss, as the pilots would take off whenever they felt like it, regardless of the timetable, so sometimes you would turn up at 10:30 for the 11:00 flight and discover it had already gone.

When our programs started winning awards in the Caribbean, I moved on to making shows in the United States, which eventually led to us winning Emmys and other awards all over the world. This was the work that first got me invited to President Reagan's White House, because I was awarded one of his "C is for caring" flags for my contribution to "Telecommunications, Media, Education, and Humanitarian Efforts."

I was on the shuttle from New York to Boston and I was ringing my assistant from one of those phones they used to have on planes, where you put your credit card into a machine embedded in the back of the seat in front of you. "By the way," she said at the end of the conversation, "you've been invited to the White House to receive this award today."

"Don't you think you should have told me this before?" So instead of going home I caught another plane to Washington straight after landing, asked the taxi to stop on the way to the White House so that I could buy a tie, and just made it, along with Peter Ueberroth, who I think was being awarded the same flag for his work heading up the 1984 Los Angeles Olympic Organizing Committee. He was running late, too.

I also got presented to the Queen of England while I was in Grenada. I was told that there could be no photographs, but I really wanted a record of this because, again, no one back home would believe it otherwise. There was a freelance photographer on the island, so I invited him to the reception along with my parents and Jim Finnegan. I told the photographer I would give him a hundred bucks if he managed to sneak a picture. He hid his camera in his pants as he was coming in and managed to get a candid shot of me just as I was introduced to the Queen. I don't think she noticed, but her husband, Prince Philip, knew exactly what was going on and totally ignored me when I tried to shake his hand.

Tip O'Neill once told me that if you can be moving your hands at the moment a picture is taken, you'll look smarter. I must have taken the advice to heart because I definitely look very animated in that picture.

It was not long before the young Grenadians who had been to college in Missouri started to return and take over the job of running of the station. To start things off I had brought down about 20 Americans to help with the launch of the station, but by the end it was just me and Larry Upton; all the rest were Grenadians returning from the course in America. One of the proudest moments of my life was the first time that I saw the possibilities of empowering people through collaboration. This is a theme that would run through my life for the next 30 years.

It was at this time that I met Deborah, who would become my wife. We'd been on our third date, and I told her I had to go to Grenada, but I would be back from the trip in a week and we would go out again then. When I got there, however, I discovered that the prime minister had grown tired of allowing all his political opponents airtime and had decided that the government should take over the station. I found myself fire-fighting to keep hold of what I had built, and so I wasn't able to get back to the United States for six weeks.

This was before the days of cell phones and the internet, so Deborah assumed I had just let her down. Eventually, however, she grew tired of waiting and came down to Grenada herself instead. It became a cute and romantic story for the kids in the coming years. It's harder, however, to make it sound romantic when similar things are still happening 30 years later. It's tough to be married to somebody whose identity is their work and who just can't say "no" to interesting opportunities, wherever they might turn up in the world. Not being able to say "no" can be something of a curse, especially when you can't sleep because you are trying to figure out how to solve a particular problem. It's always easier to keep things together when you have a loving, caring partner in the equation. I would not have achieved half as much if the kids and I had not had the exceptionally loving, caring support of Deborah.

The main tactic that the Grenadian government's security representatives used to try to persuade me to simply hand the station over was to remind me in a pretty unsubtle way of what had happened to Maurice Bishop just a few years before. In my continuing, youthful naiveté I didn't take the threats very seriously until one day I was told that the prime minister wanted to see me in his office. I went for the meeting, and when I got back, one of the local guys who worked at the station enveloped me in a huge bear hug, like he hadn't seen me for months.

"I was only gone an hour," I protested as I struggled free of his embrace.

"I was absolutely sure I would never see you again," he told me, and at that moment it dawned on me how serious things could become if I wasn't careful.

It suddenly seemed like a good idea to try to strike a deal with the government for the sale of the station before they simply took it anyway and threw me into one of the dirt-floor cells they had under the government building for the political enemies of whoever might be in power. I had been on a tour of those cells, where there was no room to stand up and just a bucket in the corner to use as a toilet, but it had not until that moment occurred to me that I could end up rotting away in one of them myself.

Eventually I sold the station to the Grenadian government. They didn't have any money, so I showed them how to do a little financial transaction where they borrowed the money against their version of the social security fund. The prime minister loved that idea so much that after I left, he borrowed a whole lot more to buy all sorts of things.

During our negotiations the station was struck by lightning and much of the equipment was put out of action. A couple of days after the storm my CFO, Jack Whyte, and I were in the water for our regular afternoon meeting, having assessed the extent of the damage.

"We need to get this place working again," I said.

"We probably shouldn't rush to get it working again until we get this deal done," he replied, staring thoughtfully out across the warm, sparkling Caribbean waters toward the horizon.

In retrospect I think he was right. They would almost certainly just have taken the station without paying, but because of the damage done by the storm they needed me to help them. We had to send all the equipment to Trinidad to be repaired, so I chartered a small, single-engine plane, which looked like it belonged to some low-level drug runner, and I unbolted the seats to make room for us and the equipment. As we landed on the runway in Port of Spain the engine cut out.

"What happened?" I asked as the pilot tried in vain to restart it so that we could taxi out of the way of other aircraft.

"I don't know," he admitted. "It just stalled."

"You mean if it had stalled fifteen seconds earlier, we would just have dropped out of the sky like a stone?"

"Yeah," he laughed, "but it didn't, so don't worry. Help me push it out of the way."

I was surprised by just how light and flimsy it was as the two of us pushed it off the runway so that we could unload our cargo.

While the equipment was being mended, we continued our negotiations with the government, asking for part of the money in advance to pay for the repairs, which gave me time to show them how to set up the financial vehicle for the rest of the money. The deal went through successfully, and the station is still running from the same building today. Herbert Blaize must have been happy with the way things turned out between us because he made an appearance at my wedding a few years later.

When Maurice Bishop was overthrown, he left behind a painting that Castro had given him in the prime minister's house. It had been damaged when the house was ransacked by angry mobs and the glass had been broken. It said in Spanish "Art as a political instrument." I noticed the picture leaning up against a wall and admired it, so Herbert gave it to me, and it hangs in my study to this day. It ignited an interest in revolutionary art in me, and later, when I was in Havana, I came across a stack of beautiful old silk screen propaganda posters which a collector was keeping under her bed in a house somewhere far down a backstreet. Castro had commissioned one of these posters each year on from the Bay of Pigs (the failed military invasion of Cuba undertaken by a CIA-sponsored paramilitary group in 1961) to the present day, and they appealed to the revolutionary flame that has always flickered deep inside my soul.

Over the years, I have collected revolutionary art from regimes as various as Castro in Cuba, Marcos in the Philippines, and Kim Jong-il in

North Korea and from both the Russian and American Revolutions. The piece from Castro is my favorite because it is another example of collaboration between the artist and the writer of the words. The adventure in Grenada had whetted my appetite for meeting other people, experiencing other cultures, eating their food and having different conversations. It had taught me the value of finding other ways of looking at things. If I had known in advance, however, how dangerous it was I might never have taken the risk, which would have meant that I would probably never have learned how to set up a TV station or how to create programs.

- It is never too soon to start your first creative entrepreneurial endeavor – take advantage of the energy and courage of youth.
- The whole world is your oyster. The best opportunities may be a long way from home – don't allow distance or cultural differences to discourage you.
- Any venture that includes empowerment or collaboration will be more rewarding.

13 | Connecting Computers to One Another

"The best way to predict the future is to create it."

—Peter Drucker

It was the end of the eighties, and Jim Finnegan and I were mulling over what our next move should be over lunch, after getting paid for the Cablevision job.

"Jim," I said, "the construction business sucks."

"What do you mean?"

"Well, think about it. We have to bid to be given the job, which is hard, then we have to actually do the work, which is a ball-breaker, then we have to fight to get paid and after we get paid, we have to start the whole process over again. We need to find a business that will provide us with recurring revenue, something where once we find a customer, they keep paying us on a regular basis."

"Agreed," Jim said, "but what business should that be?" Jim always thought better over food. He is the only person I have known who would buy a pizza to eat while he thought about what he was going to order for lunch. He wasn't fat, just tall and athletic. He was a better student and a better athlete than me. He had a full scholarship to Yale and was going to play basketball there, but he quit the team in his senior year over a dispute with the coach – all he had to do was agree with the coach, but he refused to move on principle – my type of man, a man of integrity. He had also told me he wouldn't apply to Georgetown University, as having one less person for me to compete against would help my chances. That type of honor, his balls, and his thoughtfulness made him then, and still make him, my best friend.

What sort of business we should go into was the question I was spending most of my waking hours trying to find the answer to, and which haunted me as I lay awake each night.

I had a friend who worked as an engineer at the Bank of Boston, an institution which has since merged with other banks, the venerable old name swallowed up and disappearing. My friend had an English accent, which back then made me think he must be really smart. I made a date to visit him one day for lunch and went into his workplace to meet him. The room was nothing like I had been expecting. He had a cubicle in this huge open-plan office, and there was a sea of people all around working silently on computer terminals, their heads down and their eyes focused on the information in front of them. I was shocked because I had always imagined that in a big bank everyone would be in shirtsleeves on a phone, trading and shouting and tearing their hair out. I had expected there would be a lot of noise, but there was nothing, just the quiet tapping of computer keys and the silent flickering of screens as the money moved about.

"So, more computers talk to computers than people talk to people these days?" I said when we were talking about it over lunch.

"Sure," he agreed.

"But that means you are cramming all that data down a voice network made up of copper wire, a system which hasn't really changed since Alexander Graham Bell invented the telephone a hundred years ago."

"I guess so."

"It doesn't make sense," I persisted. "That network wasn't designed to do the job you are now using it for. Can you explain to me exactly how the phone network works?"

He explained it, but I still didn't fully get it. The next two times we had lunch, I asked him to explain again, and again, and again.

"Think about this," he said eventually, pushing the plates aside so that he could use cutlery and cruets to demonstrate. "Imagine you are shipping tomatoes from a grower in California to grocery shops in Boston. The transport company picks them up from the grower and puts them in small trucks to send to a warehouse. Then a plane flies them across the country to another warehouse outside Boston. Then small trucks bring them from there into Boston and deliver them to the stores. So, you have one big plane for the long distance, two sets of small trucks and two warehouses.

"A local phone call is like one of the little trucks. So then there's the long-distance phone call, which is the plane, then there's a switch and then there's the local phone calls. So you have the California Phone Company, the New England Phone Company, and AT&T and there are two colocation facilities."

"What's the warehouse for?"

"The warehouse is where they meet or colocate."

He sat back and looked at me expectantly, obviously hoping that he had finally got the message across.

"Okay," I said, after a few moments of thought, "now I get it. But once that little pick-up truck gets into Boston, what if it has to go to five different stores?"

"Think of that as individual phone lines."

"But still. . ." I wasn't going to give up until I was sure I understood what he was saying ". . .isn't it inefficient that they are transporting data over a voice network?"

"Yes," he agreed. "They actually do have this new thing called fiber optic cable, that could carry lots and lots of phone calls and travel at the speed of light rather than the speed of sound, but it's very expensive."

I pulled my plate back in front of me and thought for a few more moments, pretending to concentrate on my food.

"If one branch of the Bank of Boston is talking to another branch," I said eventually, "does that phone call have to go all the way to that warehouse you were talking about?"

"Yes."

"Even if the two branches are right next to each other, they still can't talk to one another directly?"

"That's right."

"What would happen if I put a wire between the two branches?"

"I guess that would work."

"So, what percentage of the computers in your office is talking to other Bank of Boston computers?"

"Most of them."

"How many office buildings do you have in Boston?"

"Five major ones and dozens and dozens of smaller ones."

"If I built conduits that connected all of them, could all those computers talk to each other for free?"

"They could do that, but you would have to dig up all the streets between the offices and get a phone license. . ."

"So who do I write a proposal to?" I interrupted.

He gave me a name and introduced me to the right guy. I put in a proposal that showed how I could link all their offices and how they would recoup their investment in less than two years. They accepted the proposal and I created Corporate Communications Network, the first competitive phone company in America, to execute the plan.

At that stage, the New England Telephone Company, the incumbent phone company, had 100 percent of the market, but I started eating into their market share almost immediately, simply by building a better network. Their senior management should have realized at that stage that their old network was now insufficient for the changing needs of their users, and they should have acted quickly to build a new one. If they had done that, they would easily have ended my little start-up venture before it had had a chance to become profitable. But that would have cost billions of dollars, which would have meant a drop in their profits, which would have meant the senior managers' annual bonuses would have gone down and their shareholders would have protested because their earnings would also have taken a hit. The company would also have had to get leaner and shed employees, involving a lot of what the Special Forces would call "wet work" (assassinations), which is always unpleasant for everyone.

The incumbent senior management would have been unlikely to personally see any of the benefits that would eventually have resulted from all this disruption because it would have taken the company ten or fifteen years to build a global network, by which time they would almost certainly have moved on to other jobs or retired. Faced with the prospect of suffering all the pain without seeing any of the gain, they decided it would be preferable to find another way to crush this new, small competitor and prevent their own highly profitable model being disrupted, without making any great changes to their own system or upsetting their comfortable lives.

It was short-term thinking, which is typical big corporation behavior. The same happens in the political arena when incumbent politicians choose to make the decisions that will get them voted back in at the next election, not the ones that will produce benefits in 10 years' time, let alone 50 or 100 years, which would be gifts to future politicians and would do nothing for the furtherance of their own personal careers.

Revolutionaries can make changes for the long term because they have nothing to lose and everything to gain. For those who are already in positions of power, however, the reverse is true, and when you are in a position of power it is relatively simple to suppress the competition – or crush the revolution – simply by throwing money and lawyers at the problem. Very few start-ups can afford to hire enough lawyers to fight a big corporation once it has decided to wipe them out.

The same principles of short-term thinking can be seen in every walk of life. If someone wants to create a garden but believes they only have a few years left at that address in which to enjoy it, they will choose to plant mature trees – if they can afford that – or not plant at all. Those trees will by definition have a limited lifespan. The gardener, however, who plants young saplings and creates avenues and vistas which won't reach their peak for 50 or 100 years, is the one who is really making a contribution to the planet, to the human race, to their children and grandchildren. It takes someone with courage and foresight to labor hard to achieve results that they will not be able to enjoy themselves.

My dad and I planted a sapling behind our house when I was a kid. It didn't look like much at the time, but I had a look on Google Earth the other day, and it has grown into a giant. I'm sad Dad isn't here to enjoy its shade in the summer or watch its leaves changing color in the fall but pleased to think that all the other people who have lived in that house, and in neighboring houses, have enjoyed the benefits of his foresight. I planted the exact same species of tree at my house in Ireland for my mother's hundredth birthday.

The lobbying of the New England Telephone Company did succeed in shutting me down for a while, when the company claimed that I was a danger to the city of Boston because my network was "held together with bubble gum and baling wire." But I was more than happy to fight them because I knew that what I was doing, through empowerment and collaboration, was ultimately going to result in a better and cheaper service for the consumers, and that is an argument which is hard to argue against.

Thirty years later that company is part of Verizon, the largest multinational, telecommunications conglomerate in America, and they are spending billions of dollars a year doing the same thing now that I was doing back then, having finally given up trying to crush the small guys who dared to compete with them. It was a courageous decision by Ivan Seidenberg, the company's CEO, to commit to spending tens of billions of dollars in the face of a great deal of opposition from shortsighted shareholders. In another quarter of a century I believe fiber will be just a utility and the services in people's homes will be separated from that utility just as your toaster or your washing machine comes separately from your electricity supply.

Although that sort of nearsightedness eventually destroys big corporations, there is a positive side to it in that it allows new, small, revolutionary companies to find a way into the marketplace. If the New England Telephone Company had done the right thing in the beginning, I would never have been able to create the company that we would eventually merge then sell for more than $14 billion around ten years later. Had they been brave enough to blow up the model and cannibalize their own business, they would have dominated the phone industry for many more years, and none of the hundreds of little guys who rose up to challenge them would ever have been able to raise the necessary finance to create a new industry full of new players.

Having proved that I could set up a private business network, I then went with the same proposition to other companies such as Polaroid and Digital Equipment Company (both of which, coincidentally, like Bank of Boston, ended up going broke when they stopped innovating and other people blew up their models), and every other business Jim and I could find which had a number of buildings situated close to one another that needed to communicate frequently. Ever since the invention of the telephone, the business model for who would provide telecommunications services and how they did it had remained pretty much static, nourished by the enormous growth of the demand for the telephone and telephone lines during the twentieth century as more and more homes installed a landline and more and more corporations started to rely on the phone system to keep their businesses moving.

By the eighties, however, every home and every business in America had at least one telephone line and the industry's growth slowed down. Other technological developments were changing the whole game and the way in which it would be played was going to have to change, too. That was the moment when the big developments started to happen, but the people who had been running the phone companies for the previous century or more were bound to resist them for as long as they could.

For some time I had been working on the idea of creating a Metropolitan Area Network (MAN) for downtown Boston. The idea would be that I would own it and sell space to any number of corporate users rather than trying to convince each one to hire me to build them a private network. I had put the idea to my friend, Eddie McCormack, a former state attorney and incredibly well connected politically. He had agreed to form a company with me to develop the concept.

Once again, when faced with an impossible problem, the answer lay in partnership and collaboration.

The city authorities, however, were not keen to grant us access to the streets.

"You are not a utility," they told us, "or a phone company or a cable company. You are not proposing to act as a private contractor. We don't know who you are. We don't know whether you have the right to dig up the streets, so we're shutting you down."

I went in personally and explained how a network like this would make downtown Boston more attractive to companies. My argument convinced them, but they thought that such a network should be built and owned by the city, so it took several more months to convince them that they should let me build and own it.

Our battles were not over. In April 1989, Teleport Communications Boston (TCB), our rivals (half owned by Merrill Lynch and half owned by Fidelity), put forward a request that our certification should be denied because we lacked "the financial and other resources and competence necessary to conduct a viable operation in Massachusetts." It went on to argue that because we would inevitably fail, our "weakness and instability" would cause potential business users to avoid all alternative carriers entirely, and "to be safe," they would place all their traffic with the dominant carrier, New England Telephone. How hysterical that they were suggesting that the city should shut down their competitor because if that competitor failed it would discourage other people from competing, when people continuing to try again and again is America's secret sauce.

Fortunately the Massachusetts Department of Public Utilities did not agree with this argument and granted us the necessary certificate. What happened after that was the exact opposite of what Teleport was predicting. At that stage we were the only two potential competitors to the incumbent, who had 100 percent of the market. Today, the incumbent only has about 40 percent of the market, and that share is shrinking all the time, and there are hundreds of independent companies doing well, all copying our original model. The same has happened in every market we are working in. In Ireland alone, there are now 70 independent phone companies.

A more detailed account of this period is contained in *Tele-Revolution*, a history of the creation of a competitive local telephone industry by Richard C. Tomlinson. Dick very kindly inscribed my copy with the words, "A prime mover in the Revolution."

By holding firm to my belief that it was possible to reach residential customers cost effectively when everyone else believed it was impossible, I developed something of a reputation in the industry at the time. Reed Hundt, FCC Chairman from 1993 to 1997, began referring to me as "the Poster Boy for Residential Competition."

- However rich or powerful a corporation may be, it cannot resist progress and evolution forever.
- Always look for better, cheaper ways.
- If you have a good idea, be persistent.
- Cooperate and collaborate and be part of the empowerment culture.

THE WHITE HOUSE

WASHINGTON

December 6, 1984

Dear Mr. McCourt:

Since the beginning of this Administration, I have worked
to restore confidence in our nation's long tradition of initiative and generosity in meeting the needs of our country. I
have called upon you in the private sector to work with us
in government to find solutions to many of our social and
economic problems.

Today, more people than ever before are engaged in private
and community initiatives, rekindling the spirit of voluntarism
that is characteristic of our people. Thanks to your efforts,
our nation is making better use of our abundant resources,
and finding creative solutions to problems of human needs in
our communities. Charitable giving is at an all-time high.
You are demonstrating that it is good business to put
resources and energy back into our communities.

To encourage this favorable trend, I am establishing the
President's Citation Program for Private Sector Initiatives.
Through this program, we will recognize and honor those
businesses and associations who are making important contributions to the private sector initiatives effort. Your
organization is one of the first in the nation to receive
The "C" Flag. We hope you will proudly fly this symbol
of private sector initiative that tells one and all, "We can.
We care." May this token of our appreciation inspire
others to join you in your noble and public-spirited efforts.

Nancy joins me in congratulating you. God bless you.

Sincerely,

Ronald Reagan

Mr. David McCourt
McCourt Cable Systems
177 Milk Street
Boston, Massachusetts 02109

In 1984, I was honored by President Reagan for my contribution to telecommunications, media, education, and humanitarian efforts and invited to the White House.
As I recall in Chapter 12, I nearly didn't make it to the ceremony!

William B. Harrison, Jr.
Chairman and Chief Executive Officer

December 9, 2004

Mr. David C. McCourt
Chairman & CEO
RCN 105 Carnegie Center
Princeton, New Jersey 08540

Dear David:

Thank you for your very thoughtful letter of December 6. I admire you tremendously for how you handled a challenging situation and my admiration for you and what you stand for is even higher.

Tough times are great character tests for people and we all see that in business situations over a period of time. I have had many disappointments with people over my career but it is situations like yours that make one feel good about values and about strong people doing the right thing.

You have been a great friend of the firm's and I want to thank you for that and I want to personally thank you for our relationship.

I wish you the best and I look forward to staying in touch.

Yours very truly,.

William B. Harrison, Jr.

J.P. Morgan Chase & Co. • 270 Park Avenue, New York, NY 10017-2070
Telephone: 212 270 4019
william.harrison@chase.com

The hardest period of my career was the restructuring of RCN, the first company to offer what's referred to as triple play in telecoms (the bundling of telephone, cable television, and internet service) over one network – something we take for granted now. We owed JP Morgan $1 billion and we had a good case for not paying the bank back given our circumstances. But every employee worked together around the clock as a team to make sure that wasn't the case. Although it was a tough time, I was never prouder of a group of employees working together for a common cause and a cause that benefited others not themselves.

Growing up there were 11 of us in the house, including my Mom's parents who lived out back but were in the house all day long. This was taken at my grandparent's surprise fiftieth wedding anniversary at the house (in those days the idea of having a party anywhere but at home was not considered).

As you can see some things never change, as I'm the youngest one (top left), and I'm about to scream because my brother Frank is squeezing my leg behind my grandfather's back, despite looking completely innocent! This picture always reminds me how much my daughter Alexandra resembles my Mom.

With nine of us under one roof with one bathroom (until Dad renovated the attic with his own hands and added a bedroom and second bathroom for the two eldest sisters to have some peace and quiet), somehow it seemed normal and easy for my parents. My Mom thrived on managing a big household and never complained when we would have multiple kids from the neighborhood around the house day in, day out.

This picture of me with Larry Weinbach, former CEO and President at Unisys Corporation, was captured by world famous photographer Richard Avedon, who kindly gifted me the image despite his work selling for upwards of $50,000 at the time. He was such an inspirational yet humble man, who the *New York Times* described as helping to "define America's image of style, beauty and culture for the last half-century."

How funny that I had Jack Welch's book in my hand, when years later he would go on to be so good to me with advice.

My mentor of over 20 years, Walter Scott, Jr. (a board member of Berkshire Hatha-way and lifelong friend of Warren Buffett) has provided me with some of the most profound advice in my career. One of the most successful contractors in America's history, I've never met anyone so honest, trustworthy and supportive. I now have a similar relationship with his son Dave who is as honest and straight as his Dad.

Two years and six days after US combat troops swarmed in to restore order after the collapse of the leftist Government on the Island of Grenada, Queen Elizabeth II and Prince Philip sailed in for a state visit. I was honored to be presented to the Queen for my work founding the island's only TV station at the time, and not only that I paid a freelance photographer a hundred bucks if he managed to grab a photo. It's one I'll always cherish.

I've been fortunate to do business all over the world and meet some charming people along the way. My wife, Deborah and I had the pleasure of dining at 10 Downing Street with then UK Prime Minister John Major. When I started out as a scrappy entrepreneur at the age of 24, I couldn't have dreamt of these occasions, but I believe anyone can dream big if they're prepared to work hard and think entrepreneurially.

During the filming of our 2003 Showtime documentary series *What's Going On?*, which explored the struggles of children in crisis around the world, we were extremely fortunate to gain support from Kofi Annan, who was Secretary General of the UN at the time.

During the filming of the series, we pioneered the filmmaking by sending cameras out to untrained kids in Africa to capture their own footage. The essence of this concept was the start of our later-developed crowdsourcing technology, which gives the tools, training, and technology for everyday people to be professional content creators.

I would always try and expose my kids to the world of business from an early stage, taking them with me whenever I could, even if it meant taking them out of school for short periods. We were all on the same journey together trying to build something special. This photo was taken at a celebratory company picnic in Wilkes-Barre, Pennsylvania, where we owned the local phone company. We found it extremely important to celebrate all our successes, small and large.

JACK WELCH, LLC

P.O. Box 861
SHELTON, CT 06484

203-373-2971
203-373-2140 FAX
john.welch@corporate.ge.com

December 13, 2001

Mr. David C. McCourt
Chairman & CEO
105 Carnegie Center
RCN Corporation
Princeton, NJ 08540

Dear David:

Thank you for your recent note reminding me of your request for a face-to-face pitch.

I am flattered that you would ask, but unfortunately I am overbooked to a fault and simply can't take on any additional commitments.

Standard

Once again, thanks for thinking of me. Best wishes for a successful 2002.

Best regards,

Jack

DAVID — When you are in New York try my office and we can spend some time together late in January or Feb. Have a great Holiday — Jack

All entrepreneurs need some guiding words at one stage or another. Jack Welch, arguably one of the most successful CEOs of all time (General Electric) helped me immensely. If you don't ask for help, you might not get it. I'll always be grateful to Jack for overriding his office's "standard" response.

Our acclaimed documentary series *What's Going On?* attracted the support and participation of big names from the acting world including Meg Ryan, Angelina Jolie, Michael Douglas, and Richard Gere. Meg fronted our episode examining the impact of violent conflict on children in Northern Ireland and has been a close friend ever since.

One of my proudest accomplishments is my involvement in the long-running PBS Kids educational series *Reading Rainbow*, which was the number-one show in the classroom and ran for a hugely successful 21 seasons. In 2005, I picked up an Emmy Award for my role as executive producer. Fast-forward to today, and we're using this experience to launch a new global show which will empower kids to learn to read in a collaborative, fun, and engaging way, including parts of the world where there is low literacy.

Here I am celebrating a success with my personal assistant, who ran my life and supported me hugely through the highs and lows of life as an entrepreneur. We would always have fun along the way.

Putting that same goodwill, advice, and can-do attitude she gave to me (and the people around me) over the years to good use, she is now a successful life coach helping people achieve their goals.

ALTV.com has grown to be the fastest growing free video streaming service in the Middle East and North Africa. All my career, I've been taking on and disrupting traditional markets, and at ALTV we're bringing exciting, relevant, and hyper-local content to audiences who are increasingly shunning mainstream TV channels.

At the 2016 launch of our digital TV platform ALTV.com, we rolled out the red carpet for our international friends and partners. From left to right, we have Prince Bandar Al Saud (Co-Founder at Crescent Technologies), me, Pat Breen (Irish Minister for Employment and Small Business), Omar Talib (also Co-Founder at Crescent Technologies), and Hollywood actor Omar Miller (or "Big O," as I affectionately call him).

When I started RCN, the first-ever company to offer triple play (the bundling of telephone, cable television, and internet service), an early partnership was with utility boss Thomas May (right), who was CEO at Boston Edison at the time. By thinking differently to the major operators, we realized that we could drastically cut construction costs by partnering with power companies to use their existing infrastructure. Although our deal was done over 30 years ago, other similar partnerships are now taking off globally to expediate the delivery of high-speed connectivity.

If you've got a good idea, tell it to the world. As an entrepreneur, your ability to tell your story concisely, passionately, and sometimes with good humor, can be the difference between something taking off, or not.

Here I am talking with RTÉ radio (left), the national public service broadcaster in Ireland, and Bloomberg's UK station (right). Even when you're being asked hard questions there is no sense in not having fun!

Great partnerships span geographies, cultures, and religions. Being straight forward, true to your word, and nonpolitical means you can do business globally. All my life I've focused on collaborating with governments and other private sector organizations. The success and trust we've built comes from delivering exactly what we promise on a global scale, and we expect the same from our partners.

Enjoy having a laugh after a day of hard-fought negotiations. This is a typical Irish trait I've inherited – that we can be tough but enjoy a laugh together when the work is done with no hard feelings.

Here I'm pictured with Ireland's former Minister for Communications, Climate Action and Environment, Denis Naughten (left), and SSE Ireland's Managing Director, Stephen Wheeler (middle), and even though we're in the process of incredibly tough negotiations, we always admire their fair, forward-thinking, and ambitious approach to change-making.

I've been lucky enough to have the same deal team for decades – KPMG and Feinberg Hanson – all amazing men and woman and the best deal makers I've ever worked with (although this photo shows only men, there are several women on the team that are top notch including KPMG's Julia Klann, the best tax mind along with Mike Gaffney that I've ever worked with).

In this shot, we had just finished closing a deal and were on the way to a celebratory closing dinner at my house in Ireland.

From left to right: Aidan Golden and Michael Gaffney (KPMG), me, David Feinberg and David Dreher (Feinberg Hanson), and finally Barry Kelly (KPMG).

14

Finding a Mentor

"An educated, enlightened, and informed population is one of the surest ways of promoting the health of a democracy."

—Nelson Mandela

"A lot of people have gone further than they thought they could because someone else thought they could."

—Unknown

Anyone who tries to blow up an existing business model that has been successful in the past will meet with resistance from those who have vested interests in maintaining the status quo. No one wants to be told their Magic Goose is about to stop laying those golden eggs. Any big petroleum company, for instance, is going to want to discourage scientists from perfecting electric cars for as long as possible, just as many book publishers wanted to discredit electronic publishing when they saw it as a potential threat to printed books, and the folks who made their living from selling and developing photographic film did not welcome the birth of digital cameras.

It was not altogether surprising, therefore, when New England Phone threatened a lawsuit and filed an official complaint with the city council to say that I couldn't run a phone company and that I should be shut down. But their argument failed to convince the relevant authorities because the time was right for things to change. A trend was getting under way and no one could stop it, no matter how much money and how many lawyers they threw at it.

There are some trends which cannot be stopped, like the motor car, the television, and the smartphone; from lawn mowers to air travel, there are certain ideas and products which are just so appealing to people that demand will eventually outweigh all the difficulties that face them during development and roll-out. Cars needed well-surfaced roads in order to fulfill their potential and air travel needed mind-blowing amounts of research and development. The complexity of the modern road system would have been as incomprehensible to people 200 years ago as the idea of aircraft big enough to carry 700 people journeying from London to Sydney in less than 24 hours. But enough people wanted to travel by car and plane for the work to be done and the seemingly impossible to be achieved.

Once I had overcome the legal threats from the incumbent, I received a visit from Jim Crowe of Peter Kiewit and Sons, a world-famous engineering and construction firm in Omaha, Nebraska, who were building something called Metropolitan Fiber Systems in Chicago. Metropolitan had basically gone broke. The contractor had foreclosed on the asset, and Peter Kiewit and Sons now found themselves the proud owners of a private phone company in Chicago by accident. By that time, we were two of only three private phone companies in the country (the third one was Teleport).

Jim Crowe, one of the straightest and frankest guys I have ever had the pleasure of doing business with, wanted to know if I would consider joining forces with Kiewit. I was still only three years out of college, and I was up for every interesting opportunity that came my way.

He took me to Omaha to meet Walter Scott, the CEO and chairman of Kiewit, one of the largest and most successful privately owned contractors in America. Walter was as legendary for his personal honesty and integrity as he was for the size and consistency of his company's profits. When I told him that I had two offers he didn't try to push his.

"When making a decision," he advised me, "think to yourself, if it goes bad, will you still be better off for the decision that you made and the people you met? If the answer is 'yes,' then that's your partner. If 'no,' then thanks for your visit and it was nice to meet you."

Once again, I was being taught that collaboration was one of the keys to success.

The meeting was scheduled to be 30 minutes. It started five minutes early and ended five minutes early, as all Walter's meetings do. We went into negotiation, and I also started negotiating with Teleport with a view to eventually merging my company into one or another of them. In the end I made a deal with Kiewit, which allowed me to get back the money I had in Corporate Communications Network and also left me owning a percentage of the merged company we called MFS–McCourt.

Once we had permission we went ahead, and it wasn't long before I started receiving a stream of instructions from MFS, which I wasn't happy with, and I let my feelings be known to others. At 11:00 one night I received a call from Jim Crowe, and I started to sound off about how I felt. "Let me make one thing clear," Jim interrupted my furious monologue, "you are *my* partner in this deal. You're mine and I'm yours. If you have any issues with this deal talk to *me*." I knew at that moment that everything was going to be just fine.

Together we went on to build networks all over the country. We eventually went public and in 1997, less than 10 years after the merger, we would sell the company to MCI/WorldCom for $14.6 billion. The telecommunications world had moved on a long way in that intervening decade. Right from the beginning, I had been trying out the idea of setting up a competitive phone company on anyone I could get to sit still long enough to listen. I am a great believer in trying out ideas on as many people as possible, just as comedians will hone their jokes by testing them on audiences and seeing how they react, removing the ones that fail to raise a laugh, building on the ones that work.

When I was young, I used to believe that if I had a good idea, I should keep it to myself in case someone stole it. I have changed my view completely and now believe it is good to try ideas out on as many people as possible. It is hard for people to successfully steal ideas from you because, more often than not, the value is not in the idea itself, it is in its execution. If someone took the idea and tried to use it themself, I would still be okay as long as I made sure I executed it better than they did. Execution is always the key to success, and I would recommend anyone to read the book *Execution: The Discipline of Getting Things Done* by Larry Bossidy and Ram Charan.

Secrecy, I believe, is a great inhibitor of progress. The more people share and broadcast ideas, the more opportunities there are for cooperation and for those ideas to develop and come to fruition. If everyone is keeping everything secret, then we are doomed to keep on reinventing the wheel and will consequently slow down our rates of progress.

I have also discovered over time that if an idea is really new and you are the first one to think of it, no one wants to lend you money to develop it anyway, so it would be doubly hard for someone who has stolen an idea – and is therefore almost by definition not such a passionate advocate of that idea as the originator – to be able to raise the necessary finance.

Professional investors want to see some evidence that an idea works before they take a risk on it. "If this idea is so great," they reason, "how come no one else is doing it already?" So that also lowers the chances that anyone will succeed if they steal a revolutionary idea because how else will they raise the necessary money?

> Secrecy is nearly always driven by fear, but lack of openness and fear hold society back at every level.

Only by sharing ideas and skills have we been able to create the modern world. If people had not worked together in the past, no one would have discovered antibiotics or electricity, and no one would have been able to build roads, houses, or drainage systems. We have to work together to progress, and that includes sharing ideas and discoveries and helping one another to succeed in turning them into realities.

Protectionism has to be a negative force in the long term, even if it protects some vested interests in the short term, whether they are financial or political. Middle management in big corporations is another area where self-interested control of information can be a hugely destructive force. Managers sometimes decide to keep information to themselves because they believe it gives them an advantage over their colleagues, which it almost never does. All it does is demonstrate that they see those colleagues as competitors rather than teammates, which can't be good for the company.

The ability to share information, cooperate, and collaborate with others is one of the main reasons that the human race has been able to develop beyond the other mammals on the planet. It does not pay to worry too much about who will get the credit for things that work well.

I was on a plane once, sitting next to a guy named John Cunningham, who was COO of Wang Computers, talking about the whole theory of tying computers together so they could talk to each other, stress-testing my ideas on him while I had a captive audience.

"Great idea," he said, "but you need to simplify it. You need to be able to explain any new idea in one slide that can be understood by everyone from the most junior secretary to the most senior executive."

That was the full extent of his advice on the subject. Many years later he was Chairman of the Boston Public Library and I was invited to a fundraiser at which he was speaking. We had just sold the company for more than $14 billion, a deal which had received a lot of attention in the newspapers. We were all feeling very pleased with ourselves when he pointed to me on the front table and informed the crowd that the whole concept had been his idea in the first place.

I was reminded of a quote I saw on Ronald Reagan's desk in the Oval Office, which said, "There is no limit to the amount of good you can do if you don't care who gets the credit."

During the next 10 years, I was on the board of MFS because we had gone public and I was also president of MFS-McCourt, the New England subsidiary. MFS went on to build other subsidiaries, but that wasn't my full-time job. I also went over to Europe to build networks, running a company called McCourt Cable and Communications, which I later merged in with Kiewit, majority owner of MFS, in order to create McCourt Kiewit International, which became the largest designer and builder of networks in Europe. I moved to Woking, a town a short commuting distance outside London, to oversee the project.

It was while I was in England that I noticed people were starting to use mobile phones much more widely than in the United States. I worked out that this was because British Telecom, which at the time was one of the most profitable corporations in the world, was providing an inferior service than its American equivalents. That led me to understand that the worse the incumbent technology is, the faster the change is going to take place and the more likely that someone will succeed in rethinking the existing model. In some cases (as we would later see in Africa), the public would skip whole generations of technology.

The UK government had awarded franchises for the operation of hybrid cable-telephone networks, putting them ahead of the United States, and I felt that I should be involved. No one else knew how to build the systems at the time, so I reckoned the margins should be good. Building them would provide me with an insight into the viability of competing in the residential market, and creating and staffing a telecommunications company in the UK could provide a basis for entering the international market.

Kiewit was a domestic contractor and really had no interest in doing business overseas, but I was sure the international market presented a big opportunity and I also wanted to take every opportunity to explore personally more of the big, wide world outside the United States. I had worked hard to sell the concept to Kiewit's CEO, Walter Scott, a man I was growing to admire enormously.

In many ways Walter is like my parents: none of them says much or gives much advice, but when they do speak, they are always profoundly right. He sits on the board of Berkshire Hathaway and was a childhood friend of the company's founder, Warren Buffett, a man considered by many to be the world's most successful investor.

Walter is an incredibly good businessman, but he is never ruthless, which a lot of very successful people are. Ruthless people may make money in the short term, but they are never the truly creative entrepreneurs. They are not usually the ones who build great things from scratch, solve great problems, and have fun while they're doing it.

My wife and I went with him to Alaska once on his boat (yachts tend to be referred to as "boats" by the sort of people who own them, just as they might refer to their jets as "planes"). At night we went out with flashlights to watch the bears feeding on the salmon, and during the day we would go out to watch the icebergs breaking, chipping off pieces and bringing them back to make frozen margaritas.

One thing that I stole from that trip is to have someone at dinner pose a question to everyone at the table. "If you could come back as something else, what would that be?"

When his wife, Sue, posed the question on that trip, Walter, who owns the original Louisiana Purchase signed on sheepskin by Thomas Jefferson, chose "an explorer" and I went for "a revolutionary."

Walter is always scrupulously fair in all his dealings and I have tried to be the same. Many of the things he has said to me over the years, the "Walterisms," have come to be philosophies that I live my life by. Here are some of my favorites:

"Your first loss is your least loss," meaning that if you have a problem, deal with it immediately or it is just going to grow worse and become more expensive to fix. It is never going to go away on its own.

"Take care of your downside and the upside will take care of itself."

"Never mistake a fad for a trend."

"We appreciate your efforts, but you get paid for results."

"Bet on the jockey not on the horse." and

"Take care of your people and your equipment." (Pretty much the same advice that Herbert Blaize gave me the day we were staring down from the cliff at the fishermen and their boats in Grenada.)

"I'm not going to pay for you to go around the world looking for business," he told me when I asked if he would go international with me, "but if you can get ten million dollars' worth of profitable construction work in Europe I will partner with you."

"If that happens, we will be 50/50 partners," I replied, "but you will have to finance the growth. I don't want to have to put any more money in after that. It's been all my money up to now, so it's your turn once we partner."

He agreed, and that was what happened. We created McCourt Kiewit International and became the largest designer and builder of telecoms systems in Europe. We ended up hiring 400 engineers. One of those systems was in Dublin and, at the time of writing this, a company we own called Enet has just bought that system back from Verizon. I'm thinking of framing the original network blueprint, which has our name on it.

The rough model for most of our deals was that he would give me a little bit more than my fair share of the equity because I was doing the work. So if I put up 10 percent of the money, he might give me 15 percent of the equity.

When I bought C-TEC (a $300-million deal) we were 50/50 in the UK. I had to admit to him that I couldn't afford to do an equal split and that and we would probably have to go 70/30.

"Okay," he said.

"And also," I said, "I don't have that 30 percent either, so I will have to borrow it from you."

"Okay," he said, and we did the deal on a handshake without ever signing a piece of paper. Walter would become the greatest mentor of my career.

Business people often find it hard to believe that a lot of people in the world are not solely interested in money and will do a deal just because they like you or want to help you.

When I was just out of college, I wanted to buy an apartment that was on sale for $50,000. In those days you could borrow 80 or 90 percent of the purchase price, so I needed a deposit of $10,000, which I didn't have. The seller seemed to really like me, so I came up with the idea that he could lend me the $10,000 and hold a second mortgage on the apartment. He agreed.

While I was doing the purchase and sale agreement Nick Kensington ("Nick the Prick"), my lawyer, told me he thought I was paying too much.

"No," I said, he told me that he has had an offer for $10,000 more, but he wants me to have the apartment because he likes me."

"No one," Nick laughed, "sells their apartment to you for $10,000 less just because they like you. That's bullshit."

"No," I insisted, "I believe he wants me to have the apartment."

"It's impossible. Tell him you are going to pay him $10,000 less."

"But I really want the apartment, and he's lending me the down payment. . ."

"Dave," he interrupted. "Trust me. There's no way he has an offer for $10,000 more, and you're paying too much."

So I called the guy up and told him that although we had seemed to be in agreement, he was going to have to drop the price.

"No," he said, "I told you, I have someone who will pay more."

"It has to be less," I said.

"Don't worry," Nick told me after I had hung up. "He'll call you back in two days."

But he didn't, so I had to call him back and ask if he had thought about my new offer.

"No, we sold to the guy who offered $10,000 more, like I told you."

I rang Nick to tell him his advice had just lost me the apartment.

"That never happens!"

"It just fucking happened!"

"To be honest," he said, "the amount of work you put into setting up that deal you could have bought the whole apartment block."

So that day I learned two lessons. One was that Nick was wrong about everyone being out to make as much money from every deal as possible – that there are some people who genuinely want to help you. The other was that if you are going to go to the trouble of raising the money for an apartment (a deal) you might as well think big and use the same structure to buy the whole building (a big deal).

Many years later, before moving abroad, I went to see Walter Scott for advice.

"Remember what I told you. Just make sure that you are going to be better off for making the move even if it doesn't work out," was his sage response. "If you are, then just do it."

- Learn from the best.
- Seek out experienced mentors and try all your ideas out on them.
- Try your ideas out on as many people as possible.
- Never be fearful of sharing ideas and expertise.
- Be aware that some people truly do just want to help you out, so it's important to do the same yourself.

15

Trying to Do Everything at the Same Time

"Optimism is the faith that leads to achievement. Nothing can be done without hope and confidence."

—*Helen Keller*

"Success is walking from failure to failure with no loss of enthusiasm."

—*Winston Churchill*

At the same time as going to Europe and expanding McCourt Kiewit International, I also suggested to Walter that we should create a residential version of the MFS business model in the United States, bringing the advantages of low phone prices to home owners as well as to business owners, like MFS does. It seemed like the right time to rethink the model for phone charges to the consumer. Both jobs seemed so exciting and so full of potential I wanted to run them both myself.

"Those are two huge ideas," Walter said, "You have to pick one."

"I wanna do both."

"Pick one."

I never give up, and I hate the idea of missing out on anything that looks like it will be a good experience. It's my best quality and also my worst, along with the dogged persistence I bring to everything I do. Trying to make things work that I should have walked away from has cost me billions of dollars over the years, just as sticking with winning ideas has made me billions. I thrive on doing several things at once, my mind constantly hopping from one thing to another. Keeping several balls in the air at once is so stimulating. At the moment when my wife started going into labor with our daughter, Alex, I was in the process of buying C-TEC Corporation, a diversified telecommunications company. We were right in the middle of the deal at J.P. Morgan's offices at 60 Wall Street in New York when I had to leave to get back to Boston for the birth. They were two incredibly different but incredibly exciting events. But no way was I missing my daughter's birth. The banker was appalled that I left New York at such a critical time in the deal.

As it turned out, I didn't have to miss a thing because the banker at J.P. Morgan who was overseeing the deal came with me, and when we got to the hospital, he found himself a white coat so that he would look like a doctor to any casual passerby. He sat in the room next to the birthing room with his spreadsheets so that we could continue going through the details of the deal whenever there was a respite in the labor process. I wouldn't know how to do things any differently and my daughter, Alex, has turned out the same way, always enjoying being overscheduled and always annoyed over missing anything.

They say that a baby can hear what is going on around it from inside the womb, so maybe some of that enthusiasm for multitasking rubbed off on my daughter that day because she has turned out to be really smart, as well as being the most hardworking, tenacious, and sweetest of people. Like my father, she has an unusual capacity to be able to perform random acts of kindness with no ulterior motives, in situations where most of us wouldn't even think of them. Like me, she refuses to give up on anything and I sometimes feared that when she and her brother were wrestling, he would accidentally do her serious harm simply because she would never admit defeat.

Although I wouldn't know how to do things differently, I do appreciate that there are downsides to stretching yourself too thin and trying to do too much.

"Listen, Dave," Walter said to me one time, "you have so many good ideas – but you have a lot more ideas."

I know exactly what he meant. I am constantly having ideas and seeing opportunities for creating things where before there was nothing. I need someone else, someone I respect like Walter, to sometimes tell me "no" when I am obviously about to overstretch myself.

Knowing when to say "no" to opportunities and ideas is a problem for a lot of creative people because the "great equalizer," time, means none of us has more than twenty-four hours in a day. But saying no does not come instinctively to people like us. Creative entrepreneurs are insatiably curious about everything and about solving problems. Every problem appears as a challenge which needs to be overcome, when sometimes it would be sensible to just walk away because once you have set a new project in motion the problems and workload can snowball in entirely unpredictable ways, distracting you from other responsibilities that you should be taking care of.

"Your first loss is your least loss," as Walter would say. That is a lesson that we all have to learn if we are going to be effective.

Creative entrepreneurs, however, tend to be optimists. We believe we can make anything work, which is an absolutely critical characteristic for anyone who wants to start businesses from scratch, but we tend to forget that we only have a certain amount of time and energy at our disposal, just like everyone else, so often we end up wasting both these valuable commodities on ideas which need much more input than we are realistically able to give them. We are then forced to jump from one project to the next, when we should be focusing our energies in ways that lead to the successful execution of all the ideas we have set in motion.

Anyone wanting to live this sort of life has to be realistic about how they are going to be able to handle the workload that they take on. Just because your mind is always churning up new ideas, doesn't mean that your body is going to be able to keep up the same pace. Partly that creative energy comes from being in good shape, both physically and mentally. Physically you need to watch what you eat and what you drink and do a reasonable amount of exercise if you are going to push your body to extremes with travel and lack of sleep. If you are constantly flying between time zones, for instance, you can't expect to be able to drink large amounts of alcohol on flights or eat huge restaurant dinners every evening. You have to try to eat the sorts of food that you know your body needs.

Mentally you need to remain optimistic and upbeat at all times, otherwise the inevitable problems that come up in the course of creating a business will drag you down and you will start worrying and will become ill as a result. Two of my mother's favorite sayings are, "Moderation in everything" and "attitude, gratitude, and acceptance." I would say that by "attitude" she means "optimism," because she is the most positive person I have ever met, and all these things contribute to a healthy state of mind and body. If you can maintain those, then everything else becomes possible. My son, Dave, is like my mother. He has the genes for sure. Everyone wants to be around him because he's an energy giver, a great listener, and he has a great attitude. These are skills that are hard to develop if you are not born with them, but they're necessary if you want to sell your ideas and dreams. I spent 30 years in business trying to fine-tune these skills, but I imagine it will take Dave a lot less time to get to surpass my abilities.

We all have a finite amount of energy, but some people are better able to direct theirs into positive directions, rationing it out carefully. If you are going to be launching a business you have to be able to concentrate on that task for as long as it takes, perhaps as much as 100 percent, leaving no spare resource for anything else. A great many successful people fail to take the time to build relationships with their children or maintain relationships with their parents. You have to decide what is important and not waste energy on nonsense.

Deepak Chopra once told me that "creativity comes in the gaps between thoughts," so to be creative you have to have the energy resources to slow down and allow the creativity through, which is why meditation can be helpful for some people.

Most of us spend as much as 80 percent of our power supply worrying about what the neighbors think, whether our bosses are going to fire us, whether we have an adequate pension plan, or when we are going to find time to go to the shop for milk or walk the dog. It's no wonder middle managers in big corporations don't have enough energy resources left to do anything creative after they have been to all the meetings and written all the reports and worried about all the office politics.

The trick, therefore, is working out which ideas are worth expenditure of this valuable energy resource and which are not. I remember getting into an argument with my brother Rich over dinner once when we were in business together. I was telling him that some business idea he was develop-ing was stupid because we were both losing money on it.

"But you have thousands of stupid ideas!" he protested, going on to list several of them.

"Yeah," I replied, "but the difference is I didn't go ahead and action any of those stupid ideas. You just had one stupid idea, but you went ahead and put it into action."

I didn't appreciate at the time that Rich and I were different but complementary. So it never worked as it should have. He was a talented, proud contractor who told me shortly before he died that he wanted to be known as a contractor who did things the right way all the time, and he did.

We all need people like Walter who will listen to our ideas and tell us to move on to something else when we are heading in the wrong direction. Anyone wanting to be successful in business does have to allocate their work an enormous proportion of their time. If, however, you want to maintain a strong and stable family life, which is also crucial for anyone who wants to be successful, you do at times need to prioritize the needs of your family over business.

Six months after Alex was born, we finally got the C-TEC deal closed, having been through the regulatory process, and I was chairman and CEO of a public company for the first time at the age of thirty-four. I really needed to show up at work the first day, but I couldn't get back to their office in Wilkes-Barre in Pennsylvania on the first day because I had promised my son I would take him trick or treating for Halloween. No matter how bad it might look at work, I didn't want to miss that because I have always made it a point never to break my promises, especially to my children. That same banker called, unable to believe that I was not going to turn up again for day one as CEO. When he realized I was serious he agreed to go up there on my behalf. The following Christmas, he gave me a two-foot high hourglass. He had "always make time for Dave" engraved on one end and "always make time for Alex" on the other.

I have been lucky to have had a stable family life during the years I was building companies, and I was lucky to marry a woman who was born to be a great mother. So many people I know are forced to waste enormous amounts of energy on personal issues. Having a fully supportive family is of enormous value, but in order to achieve that, an entrepreneur has to make sure that they too play their part in making the family work. If you never get home for any of the special events in your kids' lives, and you never take the time to go on vacation with your family, you can't expect them to put in the effort and make the inevitable sacrifices either.

I loved every minute of bringing up the kids. There were times when I would sleep three nights a week in my suit because I would get home in the evening, get one of them on my lap and then fall asleep in the chair, waking up to find it was 5:00 in the morning and the kid was still there.

After that particular Halloween, the C-TEC plane picked me up at 5:00 the following morning to go to work, which I have to admit felt kind of cool as that was my first company plane.

As I've admitted, I never like to give up or miss out on anything, and I never want to choose between two things that I want to do. I want to do everything, so every month I went back to Kiewit with a new suggestion as to how I could do both the international job and the residential one in the United States, and every time Walter told me to "pick one." Eventually I came up with a formula they could live with. I remember pitching it to Walter on his private plane on a flight between the United States and the UK.

"I want to put a business plan together," I told him, "but it needs to include a study of people's propensity to change phone and cable providers in their homes."

"I'll give you $250,000 to do the business plan right away," he replied.

"I'll sell McCourt Kiewit International to MFS," I explained. "I'll put someone else in charge of launching Europe and I'll come back to the States and launch the residential service."

In reality, to have the equity and have someone else do the work is a great advantage, but back then it felt like a huge sacrifice because I wanted to be involved on a day-to-day basis in every part of the operation.

For the six to nine months after buying C-TEC, I lived during the week at the Ramada Hotel in Wilkes-Barre, Pennsylvania, across the street from the office. I kept the same room, Room 476, so I could leave my stuff there even at the weekends, when I went home, or when I was away on business. It was only when I came back unexpectedly one night and found a guy snoring in my bed that I realized the hotel had been letting my room out whenever they thought I was out of town. I went down to reception to complain and there was a great deal of confusion as to where my stuff might have disappeared to.

During all the months I was there, my wife was only able to visit once. During the visit she lost a diamond earring at the hotel, which made it the most expensive trip ever. I have a suspicion she did it on purpose, just so I wouldn't ever invite her back there again!

On the other side of the square from the office there was a Chinese restaurant. Every evening that I was in town I would work until 9:00 or 10:00 at night and then walk across the park to the restaurant where the guy would make me steamed vegetables and steamed chicken with brown rice and hoisin sauce before I walked back to the hotel. The cook became so used to me he would watch my office window and if my light was still on when he wanted to go home, he would call me,

"Mr. David," he would say in broken English, "I go home now, so I leave your food."

"Seriously?!" as my kids would say.

He would then leave it for me at the hotel with chopsticks in a brown bag. After a while I asked if he would include a knife and fork as I was too tired at that time of night to navigate with chopsticks. Next time he included the cheapest, flimsiest cutlery I have ever seen. When the company eventually moved to Princeton, New Jersey, a year later, I went in to tell him that I wouldn't be coming any more.

"Oh, Mr. David," he said. "I will miss you so much. You are my best customer."

Touched by his kind words, I settled my bill and turned to leave.

"Oh, Mr. David," he called after me, "you owe me for knife and fork."

Years later, I had a game of Monopoly designed for our employees, using symbols that were relevant to the company, and that Chinese restaurant was proudly one of them.

We had to move the company from Wilkes-Barre. It wasn't the right place for a growing business because it was too out of the way, making it really hard to recruit good people. I wanted to blow up the model and transport this 100-year-old phone company into the future, turning it into a high-tech company, but there wasn't even an international airport nearby. You had to change planes to get anywhere, making it a problem to reach New York and Washington at short notice. We needed to move somewhere where we had access to customers and to financial markets and where smart people would be happy to live and bring up their families. I put a committee together to research where would be the best place to relocate to and the place which came up as the best was Boston. I knew, however, that if I went back to Walter and told him that the company we had just bought, mostly with his money, needed to be moved back to my home town he, and everyone else, would think that I had manipulated the data so I could move close to where I lived.

When I showed my wife the research she was delighted. "So, we can stay, and you can move to Boston!"

"I can't do that," I said, "Because it will look like I'm asking everyone else to make a sacrifice but I'm not willing to make one myself."

So we picked the second choice, Princeton, which had access to New York and to four major airports. It was a great location but no one from Boston ever wants to move to New Jersey. "Hey, go back to New Jersey!" is pretty much a term of abuse in Boston. My wife was in tears at the prospect.

"Listen," I said, "we'll live there for six months, and if you don't like it, I promise we can move wherever you want."

We bought a house and we're still there twenty-six years later.

I purchased controlling interest in C-TEC Corporation in 1993. Four years later, I split it into three publicly traded companies listed on the NASDAQ Stock Exchange: RCN Corporation, Cable Michigan, Inc., and Commonwealth Telephone Enterprises, Inc. Initially, I became Chairman and CEO of all three companies, until they were sold or until a successor was found. One of the reasons I did that was because Walter and I intended to sell the companies off and if you hire a CEO for a company and they like the job, and the money, they tend not to want to sell when the time comes.

In the one case where I did bring someone in, a young talented executive named Michael Gottdenker, that was exactly what happened, and I had to interrupt my vacation and fly down from Martha's Vineyard on a beautiful summer's day to fire him because I couldn't persuade him to back the sale.

"What did I do wrong?" Michael asked.

"Almost nothing," I replied, "except you won't sell and it's our job to create value, and in this case the best value is to sell because the offer we have is more than the company is worth."

I also served as chairman and CEO of a fourth company during this time, Mercom, which I also sold. Today, the combined annualized returns of the companies spun-off from C-TEC are approximately three times the returns of the S&P 500 over the same period. Today, being CEO of four public companies all at once, even if you were the major shareholder, would be impossible.

The reason that I was determined to sell was because every year we had been growing at 4 percent, then one year we had only grown by 3 percent. I started panicking.

"It's only 1 percent difference," I was told, as if I was making a fuss about nothing.

"Bullshit," I corrected them, "it's a 25 percent reduction. And that is a reason to panic. In fact, because most of our growth is coming from people installing second lines for dial-up internet access, which is a dead product, our real growth is probably down by as much as 50 or 75 percent."

Dial-up internet was a stupid product and a by-product of Bell Company engineers trying to cram data through a voice network, and I knew it was going to die. The sale went ahead and today that company is worth less than half what we sold it for.

When I built the first competitive residential phone company in America, in Somerville, Massachusetts, Time Warner owned the cable system that I was competing against. I chose Somerville – and then Dorchester – because they were at the time good, blue-collar American towns. That fact, I believed, would make it harder for the big phone companies to shut us down because we could rightfully claim that we were bringing a phone service that was 30 percent cheaper to the people who needed help the most. That message would not have resonated so well in a wealthy town, where our competitors might have been able to use the "bubblegum and baling wire" accusation against us again. If I had been operating in a wealthier town, I would also not have had the satisfaction of feeling that I was empowering the people through collaboration.

When Time Warner, and all the other cable companies that had franchises in the towns that we built after Somerville and Dorchester, collectively tried to shut us down, calling me before the city council and giving every possible reason they could think of as to why we would not be able to provide a suitable service for the market, I merely asked who was going to go to the homeowners and explain to them why their phone bills would be going up by 30 percent. Politicians do not like to have to take messages like that to their voters. Recently we built a competitive network in Ireland, and the cost of phone service dropped by more than 30 percent in three years there as well.

I also pointed out to the phone companies that they had been claiming for years that they made a loss on each residential customer, telling everyone that the revenue they generated from their business customers subsidized that loss. So either they had been lying to the regulators about that, or I was doing them a service by taking those "loss-making" residential customers off their hands. My arguments proved to be persuasive and I was allowed to continue.

That year Time Warner was forced to drop their rates to consumers, purely because of the arrival of a competitor in the marketplace they had previously had to themselves, and it was the first time ever in America that cable rates had gone down for the end users. Every year until then they had gone up. Once again, we had the reoccurring side benefit of being David versus Goliath and enjoying the empowerment of collaboration and a gift to the underserved.

Once we were installing the network we had to once again design our own manhole covers, which meant we needed to put our name on them again. I remembered an earlier incident when the designers showed me the prototype for the MFS manhole covers and the words "MFS McCourt" were in tiny letters.

"What the fuck is that?" I asked.

"That's our name."

"Why's it so small?"

"I don't know, you just need to have your name on it."

"Okay, here's what we're going to do: we'll measure all the names on all the manhole covers. Whichever is the biggest, add half an inch. That's how big I want our letters to be."

So if you walk the streets of Boston today you will see those manhole covers with the big letters. When I sold the company, I took a few of them with me and in every one of our offices I have one set into the floor. I had one of them made into a coffee table for the house. I love them.

By rethinking the model in that way, we were able not only to slash prices but also to improve services to telephone customers all over the world. At the time when I went to Mexico and built a phone company to compete with Telmex, there was over a year's waiting time for consumers wanting to get a new phone line. We were able to supply a new line in just five days, which gave them phone service and cable TV. Almost overnight we brought the waiting time for consumers down from a year to five days. Another victory for David over Goliath.

Kiewit had introduced me to a pig farmer in Mexico, and another guy who was the largest producer of chickens in the country, and another who was a tomato farmer (when the three were together I would always call them the Full English Breakfast). They thought they could get us a license to build a cable system, but they didn't know how. So I suggested we should do it together. About six American companies went down with the idea of building cable companies, but they all went home with their tails between their legs because they did not take the necessary time and trouble to get to know their partners. Mexican business people like to feel that they are doing business with family rather than faceless business partners, so it takes time to build that sort of a relationship, spending time with their families and playing golf and generally winning their friendship, trust, and loyalty. I would take my own family with me so that they could interact with my partners' families as well.

There were a number of potential problems in the market, one of which was bad debt, so we just asked consumers to pay cash in advance; that way we didn't have the costs of sending out bills either. When the customers paid their money, we would hand them a set-top box to install themselves, saving ourselves the costs of installation. We had blown up the model of how things had been done up till then and were therefore able to bring prices right down to a level that the general public could afford and were willing to pay. Self-installs no longer sound revolutionary because everyone now does it, but at that time it was an entirely new concept, never done before.

Our next problem was how to persuade them to return the boxes to us if they decided to disconnect. I learned that every Mexican parent's dream is to build a house for their sons and daughters, and that optimism is also a large part of the national character. I discovered this when I noticed how many houses had reinforcing bars sticking out of the roofs and a local explained to me that was because every home owner expected one day to be able to afford to put another floor on the house, so they left the bars there in readiness for laying another concrete floor. I love working with people who have that kind of optimism.

So I devised a scheme whereby we gave everyone lottery tickets whenever they paid their monthly bill, increasing the number to match the number of consecutive months they had paid on time. So, when they got to 18 months, they were given 18 lottery tickets. If they missed a payment for any reason, the total of lottery tickets they had accrued would become null and void and they had to start collecting again, starting with one ticket the next time they paid. The prize, awarded every three months, was a simple house, which I had discovered you could build there at the time for just $1,200.

It worked. Everyone paid their bills and we had less churn, even in the poor neighborhoods, than we ever had in the richest areas of the United States. We played to their love of family and eternal optimism and created a win–win situation.

Another problem we had was that there were very few skilled workers who knew how to build cable systems, so we had to train people, and every time we moved to another town we had to find and train new people, which was costing a fortune and slowing us down. So I came up with a concept that was like an old-fashioned wagon train from the turn of the nineteenth century. I got trailers and would drive the trained employees around the country from Monday to Friday, providing them with a cooking camp to feed them each evening because the cost of feeding and transporting them was way lower than the cost of training new people each time. They would then sleep twenty people to each trailer. On Fridays they would make their way back home for the weekend, returning on Mondays. As a result of this idea we were able to keep the same basic crews for 1,200 miles and three years at a time. That way we only had to train a few new people each month instead of the whole new crew in each location.

Eventually, after about five years, we sold the Mexican business to Carlos Slim, a man frequently ranked as the richest in the world.

We were able to show that we were providing a service for a sector of the community that was currently being criminally underserved.

> When you rethink the model, the competition can do nothing but follow your lead, and the consumers are the eventual winners every time. Trying to re-create the story of David and Goliath can be a disaster when it doesn't work, but it turns into the story of Robin Hood when it does work.

At the time when I started in the competitive phone business it cost the consumer 30 cents a minute to make a phone call, and now it is virtually free. We were part of blowing up that model and I like to think it was a revolution. We were now competing with the big guys, and beating them.

As an FCC commissioner was quoted as saying, "Dave McCourt was part of lowering phone rates around the world."

- Know when to say "no" and walk away.
- Learn not to squander your energies unnecessarily.
- Look after your body, mind, and spirit.
- Work hard at building a strong, stable life.
- If you take care of the people that matter, they will take care of you.

16 | If You Are Persistent, Your Plan B May Be Better Than Your Plan A

"It's disturbing to people that the small David can disturb the big Goliath."
—*Beny Steinmetz*

"Those who make peaceful revolution impossible will make violent revolution inevitable."
—*John F. Kennedy*

There is inevitably an element of trial and error involved the first time you do anything. I had never built a residential phone network before winning the contracts for Somerville and Dorchester, and I was up against a monopoly. That means I was the "David" of the situation, challenging the "Goliath" figure.

We started by bundling a phone and a cable line together in one, with a homerun cable to every customer's house, which made the cable enormously thick and heavy. We then ran it across the telephone or power poles, which was great until winter brought the first ice storm and the weight became too much, dragging all the cables down into the streets. Standing outside in the bitterly cold January air, looking at my life's work to date lying on the snowy sidewalk, I realized we were going to have to redesign it with more of a "hub and spoke" architecture.

Even though we made some mistakes, however, our thesis about the future trend of private phone companies was right, and so the project still worked out with the new adjustments. We had identified a trend that was ultimately unstoppable, however many stumbles and setbacks there might be along the way.

Creative entrepreneurs always need to be ready to adapt when problems or obstacles arise. Not only had we identified the right trend, we also had a strong enough operational plan to solve all the problems as they arose – and problems did arise, as they always do.

As I looked at the two bundles of black cables lying in the snow, I realized that although I had saved on the building costs by combining the two lines, I still had two sets of operating costs. That was what drove me to work out how we might be able to run voice and internet data down the same line, using fiber, saving on building costs, cutting the weight of the cable and halving the operating costs, all at the same time. If the cables had not fallen off the poles I would never have come up with that solution.

I had actually been in the competitive telecoms business for 10 years before the government passed an act that allowed there to be competition in 1996, and that act only mentioned the word "internet" twice, both in irrelevant spots, even though we were at the height of the crazy dot-com boom by then. Things in the real world were starting to move so fast that any new regulatory act was bound to be outdated by the time it was drafted, and that was the case here, as is usual in government, no matter what country you are operating in.

| Where there is regulatory, consumer behavioral and technological change all at once, you will find opportunity.

All our ad campaigns had been constructed around the concept of the telecoms "revolution" now being well and truly under way. We bought giant billboards in New York's Times Square, showing pictures of Lenin's statue being toppled to make way for a new regime, a noose around its neck and the tag line, "No empire lasts forever; especially one that keeps you waiting five hours for a repairman."

It was not that long ago that when you called and asked for a cable or phone installation, they would tell you that they would get to you "next Wednesday" and you would have to take the day off work and wait in all day. If they then didn't manage to get to you by the end of the day, you had to repeat the entire process.

We were now making a marketing asset out of the idea that we were the revolutionaries blowing up the big boys, and the consumers responded well because we were giving them exactly what they wanted, not just what we wanted to give them.

In RCN's 1997 Annual Report, I wrote: "Once they ruled the earth. But a cataclysmic change occurred, and the dinosaurs couldn't adapt. They died. An evolutionary dead end. Something similar is under way in the telecommunications industry. A shift as profound and far-reaching as the transformation from horse and buggy to the automobile. . .the telegraph to the telephone." I was hoping to deliver a stirring revolutionary message. We held an investor meeting that year in the American Museum of Natural History in New York, under a fifty-foot Tyrannosaurus Rex.

When I launched RCN Corp (as in "Residential Communications Network"), the first residential company in the country to bundle data, voice, and video over one network, I raised $6.1 billion start-up money. That meant that I held the record for the most start-up money ever raised for any single project (a record which I think still holds today). I also got another record for the most money ever raised from an individual, ($1.65 billion, which I persuaded Microsoft founder Paul Allen to invest).

Early on it was hard to convince some of the Kiewit directors, all red meat-eating guys from Omaha, that they should move from the construction business to residential cable television by purchasing C-TEC in partnership with me. This deal was going to mean working through not only regulatory and construction issues such as engineering problems, marketing problems, and provision of service problems, but we would also have the expense of acquiring content, which would mean dealing with entertainment corporations like HBO, Showtime, and ESPN. This would be the second time I had got into the content business (the first being founding the station in Grenada) and I was excited at the prospect, but not everyone shared my enthusiasm. When I handed in the business plan for the acquisition financing to the board I had to wait nervously outside while they discussed it.

As Charlie Campbell, the vice-chairman of Kiewit put it at the time: "Jeez, maybe when you buy the company you should call it DGH – Dave Goes Hollywood. And maybe you can get that crazy guy from Atlanta to be your partner." (He was referring to Ted Turner.)

For a long time it didn't look like things were going to go my way, but I later discovered that after the crucial meeting, when the final decision was going to be taken, and was not going my way, another senior Kiewit executive, Jim Crowe, pulled Walter aside and told him he had faith in me.

"Then I'll hold you responsible if anything goes wrong," Walter replied and, despite their reservations, they approved the plan. I will forever be grateful to Jim Crowe for his support. The partnership to buy C-TEC turned out to be great and worked out for all of us.

I used some of the most creative financial engineering Wall Street had ever seen using the Reverse Morris Trust Tax-Free Spin to create a series of public companies, one of which was called Residential Communications Network (RCN). The Reverse Morris Trust is a transaction that combines a divisive reorganization with an acquisitive reorganization to allow a tax-free transfer of a subsidiary. It allowed us to spin three separate public companies out of one public company without incurring unnecessary corporate tax penalties to the shareholders, so that each company could then deploy capital and hire people in their own specific area of expertise. It made it possible for us to go on to create 12,000 new jobs, and I found myself CEO of four public companies simultaneously – something, as I mentioned earlier, that could never happen today.

The idea for RCN went from being a good plan to being a phenomenal plan. I was enormously bullish, even brash, about the future. The existing cable system operators hated me because I was openly criticizing the cable bundle and vowing to knock $20 billion off their market capitalization with our initiatives – which turned out to be an understatement. I am quoted in Dick Tomlinson's book *Tele-revolution* as accusing them of being "a bunch of crybabies" (https://books.google.co.uk/books?id=t5UiBM7DMm0C&pg=PA331&dq=david+mccourt+telecom+revolution&hl=en&sa=X&ved=0ahUKEwjvpeyWzPrgAhUPxIUKHflQCCYQ6AEIMzAC#v=snippet&q=crybabies&f=false).

It was an enormous challenge and I loved everything about it, but we still messed up very publicly indeed.

I had created another project that was now highly visible, stories of our progress appearing on the front page of the *Wall Street Journal* at least once a week. So when it went wrong it was a very public embarrassment. At the turn of the millennium, *New York* magazine ranked Paul Allen's investment the "best deal of the millennium" and the "worst deal of the millennium" in the same issue, "best" on my side and "worst" on Paul's side. To be number one on both lists seemed like a bit of a mixed achievement. It's the only time that has ever happened.

We determined that 4 percent of America's geography, the area located between New York and Washington, contained roughly 20 percent of its telecoms traffic. We worked out that whereas nationally the average reach was 30 homes per mile of cable plant, between those two cities the average rose to a staggering 150 homes per mile, giving us five times as much revenue potential for whatever capital we invested in plant.

I then became overly enamored with the idea, having successfully raised the $6 billion, and started building in Denver, Dallas, San Francisco, and Los Angeles, all the great cities of America. This was our biggest mistake. I have always been a great believer in thinking big. If an idea is good, why not scale it up? What I had not anticipated, however, was that the capital markets would then shut down because of the dot-com bust and we would suddenly be struggling to raise capital to get rid of our debt.

We converted a couple of billion dollars into equity and we were down to about three and a half billion of debt when we ran out of runway and had to turn it all into equity. Luckily for me and Walter, we were debt holders as well as equity holders, so we weren't hit as badly as some people, including Paul Allen. A year later, however, the company was back on its feet.

My mistake did not lie in taking on all the debt in the first place; rather it was because I expanded too fast. I should have stuck to the segment between Boston and Washington. I was "thinking big," which is a good thing, but I did not have an execution plan in sync with my vision, which is a bad thing. It was a mistake I made more than once.

Paul Allen forgave me, knowing that I have never done a deal in my life where I haven't put my own money in first, or where I have taken my money out first. The value of my stock in RCN was about a billion dollars, but I walked away with zero, just like everyone else. Losing the money, however, was not the saddest part. The saddest part was being forced to lay off thousands of good people.

No one likes a guy who makes money when everyone else loses, simply because he possesses information that they don't have and that he fails to share. To have a sustainable career in business you need to build a reputation among the people you want to do deals with in the future, for having always been consistent when it came to being fair and honorable in the past. If people trust you, then they will be willing to do deals on a handshake. If you get a reputation for doing side deals all the time, or for protecting your own investments ahead of theirs, people will be wary of doing business with you. I understood this sort of thing instinctively, but knowing Walter cemented it in my mind as the right way to live and the right way to do business. I would never do a side deal and I know that Walter would be incapable of ever doing the wrong thing and he would be disappointed if I ever did. The last thing I would want to do is disappoint the man who has been like a father to me.

When MFS went for an IPO two years after buying out three founders, two of those founders sued us, accusing us of knowing at the time of doing the original deal that we were going to be going public, deliberately deceiving them so we could buy them cheap. There was no way we could have known that we were going to do that, so we had no reason to pay up, but Walter said to give a million dollars to each of the three individuals.

"But only two of them are suing us," I protested. "How would we have known we were going to do an IPO years in advance, and at what price?"

"You are right, Dave, they are wrong," he agreed. "But we can't give the money to the two guys who are wrong and not give anything to the one who is acting honorably and not suing us." So we wrote three checks as instructed. That was typical of Walter's style, which always echoed the way I had been brought up. "Anybody you meet in life," my mother used to tell me, "you need to be able to look them in the eye and know you took the high road."

One of the greatest secrets of success, however, is being able to pick yourself up when you are knocked down and to be willing and able to dust yourself off and start again. Twelve of my senior managers went on to become CEOs. One of them, Mark Haverkate, writes to me every Christmas and still thanks me for the opportunity I gave him by pushing him to do things that he never knew he was capable of doing, things which he assures me enriched his life, although he definitely didn't think so at the time.

Walter and I are still partners more than 25 years later, despite going through the meat grinder together on that deal, which says a lot about both of us, and a lot about the durability of good relationships.

- Don't be afraid of learning by trial and error.
- If you fail, just pick yourself up and start again.
- Develop a reputation for being consistently fair and honorable.
- Always have a thought-through execution plan before taking any action.

17 | Crowdsourcing Is the Future

"When you have a concentration of power in a few hands, all too frequently men with the mentality of gangsters get control. History has proven that."

—Lord Acton

"The future belongs to crowds."

—Don DeLillo

At the same time as building the various telecoms corporations, I was always looking for television projects that I could get involved with after the excitement of starting the station in Grenada.

I produced the TV show *Reading Rainbow* once I was back in the United States, which was designed to help kids learn to read over the summer vacation and broadcast by the traditional networks. It had been created before me and was the oldest running educational show when Lancit Media, which owned the production company, went broke. I read about it in the *Wall Street Journal*, and on the same page of the paper it talked about the number-one kids show being the cartoon series *Beavis and Butt-Head*. I was appalled. I wasn't a good reader as a child, and later I could see that my daughter, Alex, and many of her friends also struggled with it. My father had

145

been a slow reader, too. Even now I find I am slow because I always have a pen and make notes all over the book, plus the things I am reading always stimulate other thoughts and I find my mind wandering to other things. I don't think I am that unusual in finding it was hard to read as a youngster.

I thought the balance needed redressing in favor of the kids who wanted to use their imaginations and to explore books and ideas away from the *Beavis and Butt-Head* image of kids sitting on couches saying dumb things. I bought Lancit Media and I also bought JuniorNet, which was one of the first media-technology companies, with the idea of putting them together and updating the show using the new concept of "the internet." I knew that tablets and laptops were coming down the line and that would mean we could make the show more interactive, but PBS, who had been broadcasting the show, didn't want to do that. As I was a guy of perseverance, I tried unsuccessfully for a decade to persuade PBS to let me produce a new current version. Now, years later, I am producing a number of shows with similar content which PBS could have done themselves if they had been willing to change with the times.

Eventually the PBS format started to look slow and outdated, so we are rethinking the concept. Our new show will be faster, fully interactive, and global so that it will appeal again to the big sponsors. We are doing it in partnership with Loutfy Mansour, a very smart Egyptian man living in London. Loutfy is about the same age now as I was when I first bought Lancit Media and has two young kids as I did at the time. Loutfy has the energy and smarts to totally rethink the children's entertainment business if he chooses to.

Reading is an incredibly important part of everyone's education and development. Warren Buffett has been quoted as saying that he spends 80 percent of his time reading. When he first became an investor, he read every annual report for every public company on the stock exchange, and still does so today. His belief is that in order to invest wisely, you really have to understand what is going on in the companies you are investing in. A young man recently asked him for advice on how to follow in his footsteps.

"Read every annual report," Buffett told him.

"But Mr. Buffett, there are over 400 percent more reports than when you started out."

"Start at the 'A's'," Buffett replied.

> One of the most important skills needed for success is to be able to communicate your vision to others in order to sell it, and reading will help to hone those skills because you will see how other people shape stories and messages to make them easy for people to understand.

Reading is a great way for people to learn about the world even if they aren't able to travel that much. More reading inevitably leads to less bigotry and more understanding of the nuances of different cultures and languages. You understand other people better once you have read what they have to say. You can go anywhere if you can read intelligently, and that is particularly important for anyone who wants to be successful in business.

In any business, being able to shape and tell the story of where you are going to go and being able to describe how you are going to get there is probably 80 percent of your job. Other people cannot envision what is in your head on their own; they need you to bring it alive with your words. A financial statement is really a story put into a numerical format, just as an architect's drawing is really telling an engineering story, but both these stories need to be understood by people who are not financial analysts or engineers if they are to be involved in executing your vision and turning it into a reality.

Telling stories can also be fun. When my son came home from school with a book called *Miracle's Boys* by Jacqueline Woodson, a story about biracial brothers growing up in Harlem, we bought the rights and we made a six-part mini-series for Nickelodeon, the cable and satellite television network. It was directed by Spike Lee. It could have run for much longer, but I think I probably charged Nickelodeon too much for it and they didn't make any money, even though it was very successful. It was really enjoyable to make and a great experience being on the streets in Harlem when white faces were still a pretty rare sight, just before the area started to become more gentrified.

"Hey, my Scandinavian brother," a street hawker called out to me one morning, a name which friends from that time still use for me today.

I have always been attracted to the idea of creating content which is relevant to audiences who are not well served by the mainstream program-makers, most of whom reside in places like Los Angeles, London, and

New York and have little idea of what people in places like Africa or the Middle East actually want to watch. I also like the idea of bringing stories back from those places to show to Western audiences.

In 2003, when I was producing a series on Showtime called *What's Going On?* the plan was to go out on location to parts of the world where there were real problems like HIV/Aids, hunger, or massive refugee settlements. We wanted to meet real kids in the places where they lived and allow them to tell their stories to the cameras. These were people from the lowest end of the five billion have-nots, people who would seem to have no chance to proactively make their voices and their stories heard by the rest of the world. They are also the people we most need to understand so that we can find ways to lift them up and make their lives better.

We started the ball rolling by contacting Kofi Annan, who was secretary general of the UN at the time and pitching the idea to him. Whether they lived in Sierra Leone, Brazil, or India, the series was going to show the shared experiences of children in crisis situations. To attract TV networks and viewers, I wanted well-known UN goodwill ambassadors and celebrities like Angelina Jolie, Meg Ryan, Danny Glover, and Michael Douglas to host each half-hour episode on a specific topic by getting to know the child in his or her own world. Kofi Annan made the first introductions, and once I had one celebrity on board, I was able to leverage that name to tempt the others to join us. It was a hugely successful, award-winning TV series.

My biggest regret from that project is that we had all those huge names involved and we didn't send a photographer along with them so that we could create a coffee table book once the filming was complete. Television documentaries are ephemeral things, disappearing into the ether almost as soon as they have been aired, and sometimes you need to do something deliberate to create a longer-lasting effect. A book provides something solid which can be given as a gift to those who need to feel the message we were passing on more easily than a recording of a series of programs. I won't make that mistake again.

Toward the end of the series, we were running out of budget and we had to think of a new way of doing things in order to save money. I had the idea of getting the kids themselves to participate in the filming. We fedexed cameras out to schools in Africa, asking the head teachers to give them to kids and to encourage them go out and shoot B-roll. (B-roll is supplemental or alternative footage, which is then intercut with the main shots to provide variety and background material.)

Everyone I spoke to about the idea thought I was mad. They told me I couldn't do that because what did untrained kids know about shooting with cameras? My reply to that was that although all the guys in Hollywood think they are really smart at shooting interesting footage, actually it isn't that hard. It's in the storylines and editing that the genius lies.

Hollywood's business model was created by the people in America, mostly immigrants, who invented the movie industry and went on to invent video as entertainment. The industry is so successful it operates a trade surplus with every other country in the world, but, like all giant businesses, the people at the top cannot see that the model is changing and soon they will be left behind. More video entertainment is exported from America to every single country than is imported, so it is unarguably still a highly successful industry and as a result, after four generations, everyone in Hollywood has convinced themselves that they are the most creative people in the world and cannot be replaced by amateurs.

The movie business, however, is not like Silicon Valley where you start with an engineer and then build other businesses around him or her, resulting in a very sophisticated ecosystem of angel investors and venture capitalists, support staff and private equity, which is hard to break. Hollywood is actually just a bunch of ideas and professional movie people who believe they have a monopoly on creativity and that America, particularly the West Coast, will always retain its position of dominance in the world's entertainment business. No one, and no business, should ever believe that they are going to last forever, and today's video entertainment model is no different.

Technological advances in the rest of the world have now given us the ability to blow up that 100-year-old Hollywood model. Anyone, including a barefoot kid in Africa or someone in rural Ireland, with a camera and an internet connection can now make their own programs. The Hollywood model is being eaten away just as the record companies' model was eaten away by downloads, and just as Kodak's photographic film business was eaten away by digital cameras and smartphones. Eventually the ability to make content for movies and television will be as ubiquitous as the ability to shoot and distribute photographs, and the people at the top of Hollywood have no idea that the change is coming or what it will mean to their livelihoods.

Our plan is to give people the tools to do the job of producing high-quality content and pay them right away for the content they produce that gets used. Anyone who has a particular skill can collaborate with other individuals who possess other skills, like editing and distribution, to create a final product that the public will want to watch and for which they will sometimes be willing to pay, or which can support advertising sponsorship.

"They'll steal the cameras," was the next prediction from those who couldn't understand what I was talking about.

"Who gives a fuck?" I responded, explaining that we were giving them the cameras to keep, and it was still going to be a lot cheaper than sending teams of highly paid Western movie professionals to Africa. There is no longer a need for transporting vast amounts of equipment around the world at colossal expense when entire movies can be shot entirely on smartphones. It won't be long before big movie cameras are going to look as archaic as steam engines or as archaic as cameras that stand on tripods and require the photographer to be underneath a black cloth and the subjects to be standing still for several minutes.

The footage duly came back, and we used it in all our documentaries, paying the kids according to the revenues each of the programs generated and according to how much of their footage we used. Thinking differently about how to shoot B-roll led to us developing the concept of ALTV, an app for crowdsourcing movies from all over the world on an ongoing basis, connecting the movie-making professionals with locals in any location they want to investigate and see inside. ALTV has become one of the fastest growing free streaming services in the world.

> The idea is to use art to unite cultures, to give voices to the forgotten, as we observe the process of creating the paintings.

We are also producing *What if. . .?* a documentary series following the journeys of six artists from diverse regions of the Middle East and Northern Africa who are going to be painting common canvases, with common themes and interpretations of their surroundings, exploring the largest displacement of human beings since the Second World War. There are over

65 million refugees in the world at the time of this writing and they all have something they want to say.

The traveling canvases are followed as characters in the documentaries, transported between regions, across borders and rough terrains within these unstable territories, and ending in a number of pop-up exhibitions of the resulting works in major cities like London.

We are also working on a show based on the concept of "what if we all could read?" a new reading series nothing like the old *Reading Rainbow* but based on our experience of producing the original show, which was so successful for us. It is an updated and fresher show about empowering learning and collaboration, aimed at kids in places like the Middle East. I often hear that at the moment the average American child between six and nine years of age reads for 10,000 minutes a year, while the average Middle Eastern child reads for less than 10 minutes a year. Who knows the exact fact, but I'm sure it's directionally correct. Saudi Crown Prince Mohammad bin Salman and Dubai's Sheikh Mohammad bin Rashid Al Maktoum are two thoughtful Middle East leaders who are trying to change that, let's hope they do. There is a huge potential for helping kids to raise their game.

In June 2016 we launched ALTV.com to bring video content to underserved areas of the world including the Middle East and North Africa, with expansions soon planned for South America and sub-Saharan Africa, giving millions of younger viewers access to local, high-quality content that reflects their culture, interests, and aspirations rather than programs made in a First World country where everything about the culture is different. There are only so many glossy American soap operas and game shows that someone in an African village wants to watch before they start to crave material that reflects their own daily lives and the real world they know and live in.

My contention is that there is a lot of material out there made to BBC and Hollywood standards, and now even more made to YouTube standards. While people enjoy the high standard movie-making, they are also entertained and informed by the YouTube content. I want to fill the enormous gap between these two extremes, bringing the quality of YouTube content up toward that of the BBC and Hollywood. What I am aiming for, ideally, is to find BBC quality content at YouTube prices.

At the beginning, the guys doing the execution work at ALTV tried to tell me it was not possible, but I'm certain it is. They also told me it would be impossible to pay the kids immediately for their contributions, but I'm sure that is possible too, if we just get used to the idea.

If you had told people in 1900 that one day there would be millions of cars driving around at speeds of up to 70 miles per hour at all hours of the day and night, no one would have believed it was possible. Driving was seen as a highly skilled and dangerous activity. Even the professionals didn't get much above 30 miles per hour, and then only on designated stretches of road. But the cars became more sophisticated, the road infrastructure was created and the majority of the population in the West learned to drive. If that can happen with something as complex as building and driving cars, it shouldn't be hard for huge numbers of people to learn to shoot professional-level film footage on the smartphones which they are already comfortable using as part of their daily lives.

There is a growing audience that is increasingly shunning traditional television channels in favor of more relevant, locally made content designed to be watched on smartphones and tablets. These are the people we will be reaching out to. We will be collaborating with presenters and producers in each region, nurturing talent through training, supplying facilities, and responding to whatever consumers want. The older I get the more I narrow my focus to work that empowers people through collaboration.

The results can be dramatic when you put cameras into the hands of amateurs who are actually on the ground. When Michael Douglas was on a water break while filming his episode of the *What's Going On?* series, which was developed in partnership with the United Nations, one of the kids we had given a camera to was shooting at the moment when another kid, who they had been talking about because he was one of the thousands who had been kidnapped and turned into child soldiers, just walked back into the village. The kid with the camera kept filming at the moment when the missing kid's mother saw her lost son for the first time in years. The chances of spontaneously capturing a moment like that with a professional camera crew are very slight, but we did it by rethinking the situation and empowering a local kid to help us.

I later saw Michael Douglas on a chat show with his father, Kirk, talking about this experience, saying it was one of the most meaningful things he had done up to that point in his life. "I didn't know you just did that," Kirk said, turning to look at him. "I'm proud of you."

What's Going On? won a lot of awards, showing that it is more than possible to make professional level movies with amateur footage, and now with ALTV, we are embracing the power shift toward crowdsourcing to enable the millions who want to use video cameras to talk to the world. Everyone has a story to tell and uploading it makes your narrative available across the entire globe.

By creating an app which will teach people who are currently disempowered, either because they are refugees or simply poor or unemployed, how to make content for themselves; how to edit and shoot and subtitle, we are changing the movie-school model and allowing people to reach different levels of expertise and at the same time increase the financial rewards they receive according to the levels of their training and the viewership that they reach. The material they send in might be complete programs, but in most cases, it will just be short pieces that we will work into shows. They will then be paid on the basis of what percentage of the show is made up of their material. The programs will be sold to mainstream TV, but we will also be able to micro-target advertising rather than blanketing whole geographical areas, as has always been the model in the past, and the revenue for the contributors will be worked out by algorithms and based on usage. It won't be people in the boardroom at ALTV who will decide what is good and what is bad – as happens in the traditional Hollywood model – it will be the individuals who actually choose to watch the programs.

The world will never run out of people who want to produce content, just as it will never run out of people who want to travel in private cars and communicate with one another via phones, which is one of the reasons YouTube is so successful. Anyone can upload their material onto YouTube, whether it is a song they've written and recorded or a movie of their kitten doing something cute. If it has merit, people will start to talk about it and share it and it will eventually go viral. The ALTV app works along the same principles but allows the makers of the content to benefit financially from their success.

Years ago I could see the potential of the internet for disseminating video. In a speech I made to Merrill Lynch's investment community I said: "Today video over the internet is a secondary source for primary content or a primary source for secondary content. Tomorrow it will be a primary source for primary content; that is the way it is moving." Ten years later we have Netflix and Amazon alongside Sky channels, YouTube, and Hulu.

It's all coming true, and the broadcast television model that dominated everyone's lives for so many decades is well and truly blown apart.

In the early 2000s I was so excited about the future potential for video on the internet that I invested in the first software company, called Narrow Step, that allowed full motion video over the internet and brought that to Dave Haslingden, the CEO of Fox International. Together we thought we had discovered a "talking dog" and we planned to roll it out across all of the Fox International channels. However, we soon realized we were way too early because there was no advertising model and, hard as it is to believe today, companies weren't ready for the concept. We merged it into another company because we couldn't figure out how to make money.

Today, with ALTV the times are different, but there are still a number of problems that need to be solved before the service can be marketed, including how we will task people, how we will pay them, how we will educate and train the customer, how to check the quality, and how the material will be uploaded and sold.

But movie-making is by no means the only way in which crowdsourcing is revolutionizing the way businesses gather and disseminate information. The insurance industry, for instance, is learning to do much the same thing. The insurance rates in Cairo's Tahrir Square, where a crowd of 50,000 people assembled to protest about the Egyptian government of Hosni Mubarak, doubled after the Arab Spring, although that was probably the safest time in which to insure property in the area, the riskiest time having been right before the uprising. If the insurance companies had found a way to use crowdsourcing to identify geopolitical areas that might be at risk of igniting into violence, they would have been able to adjust the insurance rates before the event, when the danger levels were actually at their highest. The more information that can be gathered in advance, the better priced all insurance policies can be. We have linked with a $5-billion London-based insurance company to do just that and we have discovered that we need to go through almost exactly the same number of steps as we needed with ALTV in order to verify the sources and the quality of the information being collected.

The principle of crowdsourcing works in almost every industry because it is about collecting accurate information from the absolute source. The intelligence community should be working along exactly the same lines, as should all the big multinational corporations. They should all be looking to gather information about what is happening at street level via crowdsourcing rather than spending huge sums of money on hiring agents in every country, and soon that will be the way everyone works. Successful revolutions nearly always start at street level and elites are nearly always overthrown, both in government and in business, because they have lost touch with what the majority of the people want. Crowdsourcing is the perfect way for them to stay in touch with public feeling and predict with far greater accuracy what is likely to happen next.

The point about crowdsourcing, of course, is that the information is gathered with the permission of the informers. It is the opposite of surveillance, although it can produce similar results, in many cases better ones. Surveillance is likely to become an increasingly controversial subject in political circles as the technology becomes more effective at gathering personal information on individuals. If government agencies, or big businesses, can spy on people in their own homes or on their private phones, without permission, they will undoubtedly gather information that might prove useful to them, but they may also engender a backlash of protest (as has been seen with the various stories that have been leaked onto sites like WikiLeaks by people like Edward Snowden). With crowdsourcing you can find out what people are thinking and doing and what they want simply by asking them.

Not that it is a completely straightforward process. Crowdsourcing has two major problems. First, how do you know that the data you are getting is real? The emergence of the term "fake news" at the time of Donald Trump's election illustrates this problem, but it is not confined to the world of news; it applies to all fake data. During the 2017 French election Marine le Pen said something along the lines of "I hope we don't find out you have an offshore account" to her opponent, who happened to be an ex-banker. It was the political equivalent of the courtroom question of "When did you stop beating your wife?" It introduced an entirely unsupported concept into the consciousness of everyone who was listening. In a courtroom that impression can be corrected by the judge and is only heard by a limited number of people. Once a comment like that gets onto social media, however, it spreads very quickly from one site to another and lodges in the public's mind regardless of whether there is any truth in it.

The second problem is how to make big data digestible. People want information that means something to them. We discovered this when we launched Findyr, an app which connects businesses with locals who have access to the information they require. It is a marketplace that enables users to make real-time information requests to collectors in over 120 countries and gather local data, perform surveys, take photos, or capture videos at any location. To get credibility for the data on Findyr we did a deal with Gallup to sell them a piece of the company because they have 80 years of experience in getting their source data right, even if their opinions and analyses of that data might sometimes turn out to be a little wide of the mark. They are the most rigorous data company in the world. That helped us to ensure that our source data was pure.

All the progress that the human race has achieved in the last few hundred years has been due to people trading and cooperating with one another. Not just trading goods and services, but trading ideas and skills as well. To make food available for us in the quantities we now enjoy in the West is not just the result of clever farming or clever cookery. There are also the scientists who discovered ways to improve the soil and increase the crop yields, the engineers who built tractors and other labor-saving farm equipment, not to mention the people who made the metal that the tractors are built from, tapped the rubber from trees for the tires, and grew the trees that provided the rubber. And all that is before you include the people who learned how to transport the food around the world, retail it through shops and restaurants, and cook it so that it is safe and digestible, not to mention beautiful to look at and tasty.

The more people there are involved in every process the more sophisticated and useful it can become. It was not possible to feed the whole world to the level we achieve today 200 years ago because there weren't so many people and they were not able to communicate their skills and ideas so effectively. Crowdsourcing is another leap forward in our ability to tap into the resources of the seven and a half billion human minds in the world and find ways for them to cross-fertilize their ideas in order to speed up progress and improve everything.

- Try to collaborate every day.
- Empower people; don't hold them back.
- Realize the potential of crowdsourcing to connect people and cultures.
- Rethink everything.

18 | The Death of the Middlemen

"Every object in a state of uniform motion tends to remain in that state of motion unless an external force is applied to it."

—Sir Isaac Newton's first law of motion

C rowdsourcing is the natural consequence of disintermediation and the death of the middleman, a trend which was largely caused, or at least exacerbated, by the rise of the internet and social media, and has been gathering pace for many years.

During the period when I was waiting for my payment from Cablevision, I wanted to buy my wife a gift for a special occasion. I had recently met a jewelry designer who made pieces for one of the most famous jewelry stores in the world. This designer explained that the store put a 100 percent mark-up on everything she made for them – which is a standard retail practice. I wanted to take advantage of the craftsmanship that this woman showed, but being short of cash I could not pay the price that the retailer would charge me, so I hatched a plan. First, I went to the store and bought the piece that I liked the best, even though I couldn't afford it.

I took it straight to the designer and asked her to copy it, knowing she would be able to do it at half the price the store was charging.

It was something of an adventure for me since I knew nothing of the jewelry business. Her workshop was up several flights of creaky stairs and behind three sets of reinforced metal doors. Once you were inside there were all these people sitting at tables sorting through piles of diamonds at the speed of light, using tweezers and magnifying glasses to identify and separate the great from the merely good. It was like watching drug dealers at work, the tables covered in millions of dollars' worth of tiny glittering stones.

Once the gift was made, I then had to go back to the store to get a refund on the item I had purchased, which meant I had to make up a story about the woman I had given it to not liking it. It was kind of embarrassing to have to make the admission, even though it was untrue, but kind of fun to play the part as well, seeing how sorry the sales associate obviously felt for me on having my generous gift rejected. It did later occur to me that if the designer's people had done any damage to the diamonds while copying the piece, or maybe even replaced some of them with less expensive ones, I would have been in big trouble. The deal, however, went through successfully, and I managed to get a really good piece of work at half the price the store would have charged.

I'm not sure this story reflects entirely well on me, but people will always get creative when wanting to impress someone they love, and it does illustrate the basic principles of "cutting out the middleman." All you need to strike a deal is for the maker of the product and the eventual customer to be able to speak to one another directly. That presupposes, however, that they know how to find one another.

The jewelry deal was only possible because of the serendipity of my meeting with the designer at exactly the right moment, but now technology allows that sort of direct transaction between the creator of the product and the final customer to happen with no more than a couple of taps on a phone screen. With the input of a few judiciously chosen words, "designer jewelry" for instance, Google will guide anyone wherever they want to go.

That is an example of the middleman being taken out of the equation by the consumer. But the same thing has also been happening from the suppliers' end of the equation. When globalization started to make every industry even more highly competitive than it had been before, every business had to look for ways to lower their costs and win another point of margin. Cutting out expensive middlemen was a highly effective way of doing that, particularly once the emerging technology made it easier for the customers to talk directly to the producers and service providers.

You can now see the results of this revolution everywhere. Where once there were travel agents in every high street, tempting people into their shops with piles of glossy colored brochures, now people book their own vacations direct with the tour operators, villa owners, airlines, and hotels online. Where once there were record stores there is now streaming and downloading. Middlemen therefore have to add another level of value to their products or they have to figure out how to get out of that business. Or they need to look for ways to rethink the model and start again. If I was willing to go to the extent I did for love, can you imagine the extent people that feel left out and can't put food on the table will go to cut out the middleman? This trend is unstoppable.

The most creative companies grabbed the opportunity by the balls as soon as they saw the way things were developing, and then took the new concepts to the next level. When airlines decided to cut down on the check-in staff at airports by putting in kiosks where passengers could check themselves in, for instance, Ryanair went one step further. Rather than spending millions rolling out kiosks in every airport, they went all the way and told passengers to check themselves in with their smartphones or print up their boarding passes at home. That way they could get rid of all the agents and get the customers to perform the whole process themselves. If someone didn't have a smartphone or a home printer then Ryanair probably wasn't the airline for them.

I was so impressed by the way that Ryanair had used technology to rethink the model of getting passengers through airports faster and more cheaply, I hired a number of technical people from the airline, including their chief technology officer, to help us launch our social media apps.

It is possible to see opportunities for taking this principle further in all areas of the economy. Hotels, for example, already let guests check themselves out with their TVs, but there is no reason why guests shouldn't be able to check themselves in as well, with their phones working as keys to the room that will be waiting for them. That way they wouldn't have to stop at the front desk at all. In fact they shouldn't need to press any elevator buttons either; they should automatically be dropped off at the right floor with a swipe of a cell phone.

Crowdsourcing has taken the removal of the middleman and the connection of customers to suppliers a stage further. The concept for ALTV was based on the idea of cutting out the many middlemen in the movie and television industries when it came to documentaries and other real-life programs, including the Hollywood distribution companies, the cable TV companies, and the guys that own the wire, by distributing content filmed by the people involved in the stories direct to viewers, but it only became practical with the rise of crowdsourcing. ALTV represents the future and creates an opportunity to put many people back to work through crowdsourcing.

Everyone can now carry a camera with them at all times on their phone, so in the end, when everyone has a smartphone and access to broadband, every piece of film taken by any smartphone will potentially be available on the internet and it will be virtually impossible for gatekeepers or middlemen to block anything in order to charge people for the privilege of being allowed to watch.

In all industries, the people who will really succeed in the future are the ones who not only know what technology can do but who also know what people want.

The middlemen can slow the process of their own annihilation down by adding new services and increasing the value of their products to the consumers, but eventually, as the man in the street becomes more confident and proficient at using the technology, they will run out of options and the trend will flow the way it was destined to go from the start: toward a more democratic, empowering, and inexpensive model for everyone in every industry.

Steve Jobs is a great example of that sort of creative entrepreneur, as was Thomas Edison. There are plenty of people who know about technology but not so many who can relate it to what people really want, or what they believe they need. Researchers who are fixating on solving a particular problem are often too inward looking, not paying enough attention to the world around them and missing the clues as to what it is that people want strongly enough to be willing to pay for it. If you don't have the ability to do this then you have to recognize that fact and either find a partner whose skills will complement yours or train yourself to be able to deal with your weaknesses. Great ideas without great execution are never more than that – they are just ideas.

Successful revolutionaries are always adept at knowing what the people on the street want, and they are most successful when the ruling elite who they wish to replace have lost touch with reality, whether they are working in government or at the top of big corporations. When organizations grow too big, they inevitably become too bureaucratic, too lazy. and too calcified, which provides opportunities for the new, young, creative, nimble revolutionaries to move in and take over. It is a law of nature transposed into corporate life.

> Decline followed by death and rebirth are inevitable; success rests on the ability to grasp the opportunities presented by evolving markets before other people see them, which inevitably means taking huge risks.

The same thing happens with countries that are looking to compete on the world stage. The inevitable stagnation and decline of the established powers provide opportunities for emerging economies to eventually replace them, although that process takes longer because advanced countries have many embedded advantages, like sophisticated financial institutions, capital markets, and recognized global rules of law which help them to stay ahead of the competition for longer. It's not hard to see, however, how the newer, more revolutionary, and sometimes more flexible systems in countries like India, China, and parts of Africa could overtake the slower and lazier economies of the West.

Of course it's not always possible to predict where revolutions will lead to at the time of their eruption because their success is always reliant on the vagaries of good luck and good timing as well as on imagination and hard work. Edison was a prolific inventor, for instance, holding more than a thousand patents in his name: electric light and power utilities, sound recording and motion pictures, all of which led to the creation and growth of major new industries worldwide. His inventions also contributed to the development of mass communication, particularly telecommunications.

> He is probably the greatest inventor in American history but even with Edison there was still an element of luck and good timing as well.

Had Edison not lived in America when he did, his inventions might never have got off the ground. If he had not lived just before the Industrial Revolution took hold, his ideas might only have been used for illumination and no one beyond a few industrial historians would ever have heard of him. As it turned out, his inventions were used to power everything that would happen in the twentieth and twenty-first centuries, from the factory lines of Henry Ford to the dishwashers and televisions which would arrive in every home after the Second World War, and the smartphones and tablets which billions of us carry around today. Henry Ford was actually chief engineer at the Edison Illuminating Company before his experiments with the gasoline engine encouraged him to set up on his own, manufacturing self-propelled vehicles.

However creative and imaginative Edison was, however, he could not have predicted all the inventions that would grow out of his ideas once other people took them on and developed them. No one knew how much they wanted the products that would spring from his initial ideas until they actually saw them and understood the benefits they would provide.

A century after Edison, when we started laying cables out across the world, we were equally unaware that the lines of communication we were opening up were going to change everything. The Industrial Revolution had sped up the agricultural world, but we were about to press the accelerator right down to the floor as the world raced into a postindustrial age.

- Be prepared when good luck comes along.
- Being a middleman is a dangerous place to be unless you add real measurable value.
- Technology is a middleman killer.

19

Ten-Year-Olds Have Great Ideas, Too

"Don't be trapped by dogma – which is living with the results of other people's thinking."

—Steve Jobs

The idea of a "total rethink" can work with the finding of solutions for small problems as well as big ones. In 1998 we still owned C-TEC Cable and each franchise had to have, by law, a local studio, but nobody ever used them because, in the days before the cable companies grew big and rich, they were mostly creepy little rooms located in the back of cable companies' offices. Each cable channel had to have one community channel that was local to that town in order to get a franchise and be granted permission to dig up the streets and lay the cables. These local studios were costing us around $1 million per year, and I wanted to find a way to rationalize them down and at the same time make the studio experience more congenial for those who ended up interviewing or being interviewed in them.

The way it was structured wasn't logical. It would have been simple for people to travel from surrounding towns to one central location in order to be interviewed or perform or talk, but I was told it was a legal requirement to provide studio facilities in each town. Then it occurred to me that instead of trying to coax people to the studios, which were depressing, sterile places, we should find a way to take the studios to the people and to the places where the stories were actually happening, by creating an outside broadcast facility that would comply with all the regulations for providing studio space in each community and also add a sense of excitement and immediacy to all the broadcasts.

"What would happen," I asked the lawyers, "if I built a mobile studio in a bus and whenever anyone needed it, we could just drive it to wherever the story is happening?"

The lawyers looked into it and came back to tell me that would be okay and we would not be contravening any of the requirements of our contracts. So that's what I did, hiring six drivers so that the unit could work seven days a week, traveling from town to town, filming at a little league game in one town, a Girl Scouts' jamboree in the next, a school committee meeting in the next, and a kids' show-and-tell in the one after. Instead of approaching the problem by making incremental changes such as reducing the size of the studios, or lowering the staff costs, or campaigning for people to turn out the lights and cut the overhead, we had turned the model on its head and made the product both different and better in the process.

By this time, the ventures I was involved with were growing big and I was having to adapt my thinking to take that into account. RCN was the first and largest competitive phone company for residential areas, and Corporate Communications was the first competitive phone company for the business market. By 2000 we were hiring 37 new employees each day – three-quarters of them for design, build, maintenance, and installation jobs – but it was proving really hard to find good, well-trained, experienced people in such a new industry sector.

I was in the car with my 10-year-old son, Dave, one day, telling him how hard it was to find enough trained people to fill all the vacancies because we were inventing an industry and there were no qualified people on the market. There was in fact no market for jobs.

Dave used to gaze out the window all the time when we were traveling, just opening up his mind and remaining tranquil, which led to him coming up with many of his best ideas. Sometimes, if I am on a plane, I try to do the same thing, but five minutes later I will have forgotten and will find myself on my phone, writing emails to be sent as soon as I am back on the ground. I still have a lot to learn from Dave on how to embrace the quiet moments, as he often points out things that I have missed because of my frenzied life.

"Because it's been a monopoly business for a hundred years," I explained to him, "there are virtually no employees on the market who understand designing, building, installing, and operating phone systems other than the monopoly's workforce. We have invented this industry. They all work for our competitor and would never want to come to work for us. In most industries there are trained people out there for hire, but we have to train all our own people."

"Why don't you start your own school?" he asked as we waited by a red light. "You could call it 'Cable Camp.'"

Sometimes the very young see things clearly because their brains are not yet cluttered up with experience. They can see the end result that is needed, and they are not daunted by all the steps that it will take to reach that result because they have no idea what those steps are. That's also why the young make good revolutionaries.

It was such a great idea I couldn't imagine why I hadn't thought of it before – but then it's the same with all the greatest ideas – they seem obvious once someone has thought of and articulated them.

I set to work straightaway, buying some land and some bucket trucks, and I hired a bunch of retired phone-company workers to be teachers. We taught the applicants how to design a cable phone system, how to build it, how to maintain the cables, how to splice and pull them, how to fix them after a storm, and how to do a service call. Anyone who passed Cable Camp would be offered a job. Around 5,000 people went through the camp. One of my favorite jobs was going out to congratulate the new employees every three months when they graduated.

At that stage we were spending about $100 million per month of CAPEX (the money to build and maintain the new networks). At our height we had around 12,000 employees, after having started from scratch.

We trained all the blue-collar installers how to sell as well, so they could upgrade the services that the customer was buying on the spot. Once an installer was physically with a customer it was a relatively easy job to upsell them. We would also pay them a commission that could make a considerable difference to their earning power and their lifestyle.

The downside of being the first in a new industry might be that there is a very limited pool of trained and experienced labor to draw upon, but the upside is that you get to lay the ground rules for how the industry is going to be shaped as you go along – you can set your own gold standards.

- If the thing you need does not exist, invent it yourself.
- If there is no one to do the job, do it yourself.
- Good ideas can come from anyone at any time – so keep your ears and mind open.
- It's a shame to be ready and not to be called – but it is a sin to be called and not to be ready.

20 | Never Be Afraid to Think Big – or to Think Young

"My great concern is not whether you have failed, but whether you are content with your failure."

—Abraham Lincoln

"Too often in life, something happens and we blame other people for us not being happy or satisfied or fulfilled. So the point is, we all have choices, and we make the choice to accept people or situations or not to accept situations."

—Tom Brady

One of the big mistakes people make is not thinking big enough. We can all achieve far more than we believe we are capable of in all areas of our lives, particularly business, but we deliberately hold ourselves back, often for entirely illogical reasons. We are nearly always capable of solving all the problems that worry us, but we have to believe it before we can achieve it.

The use of Abraham Lincoln and Tom Brady's quotes at the beginning of this chapter is deliberate. Whether you are a New England Patriots fan or don't care for politicians you can't deny the accomplishments of these two men.

Abraham Lincoln overcame enormous obstacles, including being declared bankrupt, running for various public offices, and being defeated a record 10 times, 5 of which were runs for both the congress and senate before being elected president of the United States at 51 years of age. In those days, life expectancy was only 35, but Lincoln survived to thrive in ways that only his will and perseverance could have inspired.

Tom Brady was a seventh string quarterback at the beginning of his college career, and NFL scouts called him scrawny, lacking quickness, mediocre, and a marginal athlete. However, Brady has been honored with six Super Bowl championships, four Super Bowl MVP awards (the most ever by a single player), he has won three league MVP awards, has been selected to numerous Pro Bowls, named sportsman of the year, male athlete of the year, and has led his team to more division titles (16) than any other quarterback in NFL history. These are extreme examples of people who were all but given up on – disregarded by those people who are put in a position to judge and determine people's future. The same basic principles apply to all of us – believe in yourself, never give up, and don't let other people's views determine your own.

If you have an idea for a product that will work in your home city, why not replicate it in every other city in the world? If you are going out to raise money for a project which is going to bring a service to 100,000 homes, it's going to be almost as easy to raise the money you would need to take it to 1 million homes, or 10 million. As long as you know how you will be able to execute the plan should it come to fruition, then there need be no limit to how wide you can spread your net.

Investors are always looking for projects that are scalable and that will bring big returns. Even if you don't scale the business yourself, the people who buy it from you, and who will be instrumental in setting the price you receive, will be looking for opportunities to do so. They need to be able to see that it is scalable, even if you are not the one to do it, otherwise they won't pay a high multiple on your cash flow. So even if you don't intend to be the person to expand your business nationally or internationally, still plan how you could do so in detail. Maybe it could be a franchise operation of some sort. McDonald's was just another burger restaurant until plans were laid for spreading the model out, and Starbucks was just another coffee shop. Facebook could have remained a social tool for a few elite universities if no one had taken the plunge and thought through the possibilities.

If your idea is good then it will almost always be scalable; after all, you have already gone through all the design and construction hassle, so you might as well maximize the returns you receive for your labors. For some reason people feel nervous about asking for too much money or embarrassed to claim that their idea has worldwide potential. Maybe they are afraid that if they do that and then they fail everyone will know about it. But the sorts of people who blow up the model and succeed in changing the world never have that problem. If they fail, then they shrug it off and try again. If you are going to fail it makes no difference whether you fail trying something big or something small. At the time of writing this, I am in the middle of trying to get five companies off the ground. I hope that all of them will become multi-million-dollar success stories, but in reality, I know they won't. Some will succeed and some might not, but hopefully at least one of them will be a huge success. It's impossible to know which will be the winners, but we will have a lot of fun finding out and we will employ a lot of people and hopefully do some good along the way, making the world a better place for at least some of its citizens.

If you think big, however, you do have to have an execution plan that will work in sync with your vision. That was where I went wrong with the rollout of RCN. It is perfectly possible to achieve enormous things very quickly. Facebook and Alibaba, for example, have both been good at that. They think very big indeed, but their execution plans have always been in line with their ambitious goals. They have always been focused on how they are going to achieve the goals they have set themselves.

I was on a board of the University College Dublin along with the CEO of Chubb Insurance and I read that the company had something like a 90 percent market share when it came to insuring every home in America that was worth over $2 million. It was an unbelievable figure and I asked him how it was even possible to have achieved such high market penetration. He took a deep drag on his cigarette, squinted at me through the cloud of smoke as if I was mad, and simply growled: "I made it my objective."

It was such a great answer. He had a plan and an objective, and he executed against it. Entrepreneurs are not always good at running day-to-day operations themselves because in order to be a great entrepreneur you need to be able to keep putting yourself in the future and then looking back. An operations person, on the other hand, has to put themselves in the present and look forward in order to anticipate the problems the company is likely to be facing if it follows a particular course of action, which requires an opposite skill set. Entrepreneurs usually focus on the upside while operations people need to focus on the downside.

All great leaders and entrepreneurs need to have good operations people to put the brakes on them when their ideas run too far ahead. You can see it with governments too. If you compare Venezuela, which is incredibly wealthy in natural resources but still managed to run itself into the ground economically, and Cuba, a tiny island which had no natural resources and managed not only to survive but at the same time to hold out against the United States for decades, you can see what is possible. Somewhere behind the scenes the Cuban government must have had some brilliant operations people keeping things going during the tough times. Donald Trump is an even better example of an entrepreneur who needs good operations people to hold him in check. When he arrived in the White House, he was bursting with so many ideas and so much enthusiasm he kept getting in his own way by insisting that he could do everything immediately and all by himself. Such arrogance always catches up with people if they don't let their ops personnel take over. Everyone needs to work as part of a team at some stage if they actually want to achieve big results, something that young people wanting to be entrepreneurs don't often appreciate.

I guess my mother was right about my "secret sauce" being the fact that I can talk to anyone, no matter who they are. As I've said before, all the best ideas come from talking to people and listening to what they have to say, whether they are 10 years old and just starting out on life with fresh eyes or 80 years old and experienced in running giant corporations. Everyone has something to teach you, even if it is what *not* to do. I am frequently told that both my children have this same talent. This is probably partly DNA, partly environmental, and partly because they have a caring, loving mother who always puts them first in her life.

In 1998 I started a Tech Summit at the Phoenician Hotel in Arizona with Launny Steffens, who was vice-chairman of Merrill Lynch at the time, and we would invite the smartest people we knew, including big names such as Paul Allen, Deepak Chopra, Quincy Jones, Chuck Norris, and Barry Sternlicht, who runs Starwood Capital. We would spend two days and two evenings together during the week, discussing big ideas, and then I would stay on for the weekend with my family.

I would create the agenda for those two days, posing the most difficult problems facing business and the world in general that I could think of, and getting all their viewpoints on each subject. I remember one of the topics was whether it would ever be possible to outsource labor to crowdsourcing, which seemed very far-fetched at the time, but here we are, 20 years later, doing exactly that. Also, I asked whether you could persuade consumers to do the work themselves if you lowered the prices, getting them doing things like installing their own modems, just like building their own flat-pack furniture. Only one other guy agreed with me on that one, but of course that too is now happening all over the world.

They were great meetings. It was stimulating to talk to people who were so creative in such varied fields. The only way to find out what is happening in the world, and what needs to happen, is to listen to other people. On our own, each of us knows very little indeed. When I was starting out, I often used to deliberately spend time with people who were incredibly successful and well-known in their fields, but actually you can learn as much from talking to a cab driver or a kid who's still in school, because they will force you to think differently about stuff and to come at it from different angles.

People who are really successful and famous tend to be very sure of themselves and their opinions because they are surrounded by people who are paid to laugh at their jokes and tell them they are great all the time. If you are too sure of yourself, you are less likely to be introspective about anything and eventually that will make you both less creative and less interesting. Ideas for blowing up the model more often come from people who are very young or very inexperienced in a particular field because they have none of the negative baggage which we all pick up as we go through life, but for the same reasons they are usually not the right people to execute those ideas.

You can, of course, take that too far and exhibit more confidence than your experience or wisdom merit. I was once with CNBC news anchor David Faber, and we were talking about one of his colleagues.

"She's pretty confident of herself, isn't she," I said. "No introspection," he growled, "no self-doubt."

It's a good line and I am sure we have all met people like that. But having said that, this lady's confidence had still carried her a long way. If she becomes able to access a little introspection as well, then she will be able to reach a whole other level.

It's also always a mistake to only socialize within your own peer group and age group. When asked for advice on how to achieve longevity, my 101-year-old mother always says, "Don't hang around with old people, they'll bring you down." She is partly joking, but she is also making the point that you need to have as diverse a group of friends as possible in age, socioeconomically, and ethnically, particularly to include young people with fresh, new ideas.

Over the years my mother has given me a lot of good advice, such as, "if you have a problem, deal with it and then move on – good or bad – move on." She also once told me, "If you're ever lucky enough to have a beach house, make sure it's not so fancy that people can't sit on the chairs in wet bathing suits or come indoors with sand on their feet. If you do that, you'll never have any kids visiting because they won't feel comfortable, and a beach house should be full of kids."

We took that advice when we were lucky enough to be able to buy a house on the beach in Martha's Vineyard. As a result, when you get up in the morning you always find kids sleeping over on the couches and floors, which keeps the house alive. Likewise, in New Jersey our house is the place where the kids come to watch the football games and enjoy good food and good conversation.

These young people are the ones who are going to be running the world in a few years, and if the older generations don't listen to what they have to say, they are very quickly going to find themselves out of touch and unable to foresee the trends which will provide the most successful business ideas of the future. It is the things that kids want today that will determine what the marketplace for goods and services looks like tomorrow.

We need more young people to get to the top in business and politics as well, new faces with new ideas. When President Trump started calling in the business community for meetings, I recognized them all. They were all captains of industry, mostly old, all just talking to one another. Where was the young guy who's selling milk at midnight from his store because no one else in the area is doing it? Or the young woman who started an independent coffee shop right next door to Starbucks and took away all their business because she was doing something different and right? These are the people who are having the ideas that will change the future as much as the famous geniuses who find the previously unfindable and cure the previously incurable.

Some of the old men at the top of the business world probably don't even use smartphones. How would they know what the future should look like, or how we should get there? What are the chances that they are going to be blowing up the model that they built themselves? Why would they want to replace it with something completely different, even if that new model is infinitely better than anything that came before, when they are completely comfortable with the way things are?

You can see examples of reactive thinking in every big company. I was at a board meeting at a bank around 2002, where the old guys were making a presentation about how many new branches they were going to be opening. It seemed like a good idea to them because at that moment the branches they had were making money. I know for a fact, however, that most young people have no intention of ever stepping into a bank in their entire lives because they can satisfy all their financial needs on their smartphones. So opening new branches is just a short-term way of generating some more money and maybe increasing the stock options value, which mostly belong to the same old guys. But it does not rethink the model in a way that will secure the bank's position in the future. These were operational people making strategic decisions, contravening Jack Welch's dictum that you should never mix operations and strategy. A strategic person would have put themselves in the future and seen that those new branches would all be closing in 10 years.

I suggested that it might be a better idea to build branches in Africa and getting our brand known to people who are new to banking. You could have heard a pin drop in the silence that ensued, before they moved on as if I hadn't spoken. None of the big banks took that opportunity and now Africa leads the world on mobile banking, solving the problem themselves. What has happened in mobile banking is a likely precursor for what is going to happen in the telecom industries generally. McKinsey reported in 2015 that the "Middle Eastern and African region represented 8 percent of the global telecom market but still contributed nearly 20 percent of the economic profit pool" with a mobile broadband subscriber base estimated to be well over one billion (https://www.mckinsey.com/~/media/mckinsey/industries/telecommunications/our%20insights/winning%20the%20rush%20for%20data%20services%20in%20the%20middle%20east%20and%20africa/telecommunications%20industry%20at%20cliffs%20edge%20time%20for%20bold%20decisions_june2016.ashx).

The number of smartphone connections in Africa was reported in 2016 to have almost doubled in two years. By the end of 2015 nearly half of the population of the continent subscribed to mobile services. That year, mobile technologies and services contributed around $150 billion of economic value and the mobile ecosystem supported nearly four million jobs. Cell phones, it is predicted, will account for almost 10 percent of African GDP by the end of the decade. Under those circumstances why would young people suddenly develop a habit for going into banks, which are often many miles away from where they live and work, when they can do everything on their phones?

Twenty years down the line it will be those same young people who will be the ones with all the money, and the next CEO of that bank will have to close all those branches that his or her predecessor opened. The growth of "non-bank" banks is huge and a major part of the progress being made in the less-developed parts of the world, any bank that invests in that sector of the market will almost certainly thrive in the long term, but it requires them to think big and think young, discarding much of what they have learned in banking over the last 100 years.

When accepting an award in 1963, Bob Dylan said: "It is not an old people's world. It has nothing to do with old people. Old people, when their hair grows out, they should go out. And I look down to see the people that are governing me and making my rules – and they haven't got any hair on their heads – I get very uptight about it" (https://www.newyorker.com /culture/cultural-comment/bob-dylan-extending-line).

As one of the old people he was talking about (as, of course, is he himself now), I would obviously not want to endorse every word of his pronouncement, but I think it is true that most successful revolutionaries (and most successful entrepreneurs) are young. That is partly because young people's brains work faster but also because they take greater risks as they have less to lose. They can visualize the potential rewards, but they do not yet have enough life experience to see all the dangers, making them more fearless. Fortune, as we all know, "favors the bold." If armies recruited soldiers in their fifties and sixties rather than in their teens and twenties there would almost certainly be a great deal less fighting and less loss of life. It is much easier to persuade 18-year-olds to risk their lives in a war zone than 40-year-olds who have children waiting for them at home. Boldness tends to wane with the years.

MRI scans of brains have shown that the ways in which we think change as we grow older. The association between action and effect only develops later.

| To really change things you need to deliberately think young, think long term, and think differently.

Some people are wired to have a "young" view of the future and retain the courage needed to take big risks and make themselves uncomfortable in the short term in order to benefit from longer-term gains. Most people, however, do not, and become increasingly unlikely to be able to revolutionize anything as they grow older.

If all the world's richest companies are in the oil business, for instance, is it any wonder it is taking so long for electric cars to take over? They would be cheaper to run, quieter and more climate friendly. The only real downside to them replacing petrol and diesel driven engines is that the market for oil would virtually disappear overnight.

Likewise, if you pay lawyers by the hour, is it any wonder that they make everything about the legal process as complicated and time-consuming as possible? Is an older, more established lawyer, who has spent many years working up to being able to charge huge hourly fees, likely to want to change that system? The push for a revolution is much more likely to come from someone young who is just starting out, needing to make a reputation for themselves and not yet earning the big bucks.

| All these business models need to be rethought by people who have no vested interests in the status quo and a deep interest in the future being as good as possible for everyone.

The guys running the big corporations are never going to be the ones suggesting ways to rethink the model. They are going to be the ones with the vested interests in slowing the race down as much as possible because they don't want to lose the lead they have taken so long to build up. It may well be that when they were young and hungry, they rethought some models themselves, and that was how they came to be rich and successful, but now they are likely to be doing whatever they can to slow down those who might start a new revolution which could topple them from their positions of power. There is always a temptation to pull the ladder up behind you once you have climbed to the top, but it is a temptation that everyone should resist because it inevitably leads to calcification and death.

No corporation, government, or country, however, is immune from being blown up by one new good idea. The bigger the company the slower it is likely to be when it comes to responding to changes in the market and threats from smaller, nimbler competitors. Ultimately no one is "too big to fail," not even Coca-Cola or the Roman Catholic Church, Apple or the United States of America. If the revolutionaries think big enough, they can achieve whatever they want.

So much about the current status quo needs rethinking, which means there are opportunities everywhere for creative entrepreneurs to make a real difference. To start with, there is the higher education system in America, which is producing the people who will be shaping and running the country in 20 years' time. However, this system was designed in the Industrial Revolution. If, for instance, going to a top university is going to continue to cost $60,000 or more per year, then only people from the existing top echelons of society are going to be able to get in, people who probably have dynastic reasons for wanting to maintain the status quo. They may seem the brightest people in the pool, but they may only be because maybe their families can afford to send them to the best preparatory schools and hire the tutors that absolutely ensure good exam results because their training is all based on studying previous exam questions, but that does not mean they are the most creative or courageous thinkers. The American universities are still the pride of the world, although our education system below that level is not so great. To get into those universities you have to achieve certain grades in standardized tests, which anyone with reasonable intelligence can do if they follow a set program. But that program is designed around encouraging students to think "within the box," because in times of slow, incremental change, that is what is needed. But the real world, which has sped up since the Industrial Revolution, now needs the skills of those who think "outside the box."

When I am interviewing people for Georgetown University's Entrepreneurial Award, the business plans that resonate with me are usually those where the kids have taken something in their life that they think is wrong and have tried to invent something new to solve the problem, rather than simply copying someone else's idea. There was one kid years ago who came to me with the idea of making the identity cards at the university work for paying for food in local restaurants as well as in the dining hall. He had figured out a way that the outlets could do it without investing in an expensive credit card terminal and had actually gone ahead and executed the idea. Most people who come up with the good ideas, however, underestimate the degree of hard work that will be required for execution. They need to understand the importance of luck, of finding a good mentor, of focusing, and, above all, of working incredibly hard.

When I was interviewing students for admission as an alumni interviewer, a kid came in front of me as a B+/A student. He was captain of the football team and president of 4H, which is a global network of youth organizations whose mission is "engaging youth to reach their fullest potential while advancing the field of youth development." This was the least likely combination of achievements you could imagine in the US school system. He then told me that before setting off for school each day he got up and baled hay, which he then sold. He had used the money from that business venture to buy a two-unit apartment unit with a friend.

"What did you learn from that?" I asked.

"A lot of things," he grinned, "like people don't pay their rent unless you go collect it yourself. And if something breaks you have to go fix it at the weekend."

When I heard that Georgetown had turned him down – presumably because he had a few B+ grades – I wrote to the president of the university to say that this guy was exactly the sort they needed in a business school if they wanted diversity and if they wanted to encourage creative entrepreneurial thinking.

The problem is that most of the kids who apply for university and get accepted have identical CVs. They all get good grades; they all travel and claim they were doing it to "help the less fortunate," telling stories of working in orphanages or refugee camps (for a week), so none of that makes them stand out against the competition or proves that they have creative, entrepreneurial brains. My kids were at a school in the United States that is almost impossible to get into unless you are there from the start, but I could see they were turning out just like all the others. Even the parents all looked the same at the school gates. I felt that it would be good to break that cycle.

"I think we should go overseas to go to a different school for six months," I suggested over dinner one evening.

"If we're going to do it for six months," Dave said, to my surprise, "why don't we do it for a whole year?"

"Where?" Alex asked.

"I'll go anywhere you want," I said, "as long as English is not their primary language."

They picked Italy and we canceled our ski trip in order to go look at some schools in Florence, Rome, and Milan. The kids picked Rome. Initially Deborah correctly pointed out all the reasons why this would be difficult and disruptive.

"If we list all the problems," I said, "then we are never going to make the decision. We have to put ourselves in the future and ask whether this will prove to be a good thing to have done. Then we can work out how to do it."

It was a good example of how business training can sometimes help you in your personal life. We made the decision, solved all the administrative problems, Deborah found us an apartment, and we packed up and left. The kids loved it, and most of the time Deborah would now agree that it was a great experience for all of us.

As parents, we always wanted to take the kids to places where there had been conflicts, so they could learn how things worked in other parts of the world. We had them watch movies about Michael Collins and then we brought them to Dublin, to the scene of Bloody Sunday. We took them to Cambodia after encouraging them to read about the Khmer Rouge and the genocide they inflicted while in power. We took them to the West Bank and other Palestinian areas in Israel. A week after we got home from Israel, Alex was looking at the front of the *New York Times* I was reading and saw a picture of a scene where a rocket had blown up Yasser Arafat's headquarters across the street from a café we had been eating in just a few days before. She couldn't understand why what had seemed like such a normal street a few days before could now be part of a war zone.

I also took the family to Cuba, but I had to charter a plane from Mexico and didn't tell my wife where we were going until we were on the runway.

Online education is already putting enormous pressure on the traditional education model. We are now seeing job applications from fully qualified people who did it all on Lynda.com, the online tuition service. Who needs to spend $60,000 per year on a university course when they can do it online at a fraction of the cost? The universities claim they are "tuition blind" and that they will help good students who can't afford to pay the full fees, but it's an exception for anyone to get into a position of being considered for a top university without some money behind them to begin with. My wife got very sick years ago and was in hospital for a long time. On her return from the hospital she took a break at Deepak Chopra's center in California. The kids seemed a little blue, so one day when I picked them up from school, instead of going home I headed to the airport and Disneyland. When Deborah called to check that I was helping them with their homework I had to confess where we were. I loved those times with the kids. Every year before Christmas I would take Alex out of school for a day and we would go into New York to do her Christmas shopping for her brother and her mother. She would get all dressed up and we would have a fancy lunch together. With Dave I would take him to the Super Bowl.

Putting them through the same educational program as everyone else isn't the best way to bring on the people who are going to come up with new and exciting ideas for doing things better in the future. Those people need to have no vested interest in maintaining the status quo and they need to have developed strong urges to make things better for everyone.

When I was at Georgetown as a student, 40 years ago, there were all sorts of blue-collar workers' kids there, and they often had more to contribute to debates than the traditional Ivy League students because they had hands-on experience of real life, with all its real problems. They were the ones who could see the possibilities for change as well as the need for it. Only if you understand the real problems can you hope to come up with world-changing solutions.

The teachers in any good university will all have read a great many books, many of which will have gone out of date before they were even printed because of the speed at which everything is changing. How useful is that? An educational publisher explained to me once that they produce new editions of textbooks about every 7 years, but that they make very few changes to each edition, so that means that the bulk of the information the students are studying could be anything up to 14 years old, in a world where governments can fall and new industries can emerge virtually overnight. This explains why online education is going to become a real alternative, because it is current.

Textbooks may only change every 7 to 10 years or so, but ideas are now changing from hour to hour and day to day. Just that fact alone means that the current further education model, which worked fine 80 years ago, is now entirely unfit for function in many areas. Too many of the people working within the universities and colleges actually have no idea of what is going on in the rest of the world, among the five billion people who are getting left behind. Yet this is the part of the world where all the changes need to happen if the future is going to work for everyone. It is also the part of the world where all the best ideas are simmering away, waiting for an opportunity to become realities. This is why I spend most of my time in those parts of the world in this phase of my career. Over the last two years I have been in 12 different countries on 4 different continents, including several countries that are currently not speaking to each other, such as Saudi Arabia and Qatar, Israel and Palestine.

Government information is often just as out of date as university textbooks. The US Government, for instance, spends millions on Consumer Price Index information, but if they hired us to crowdsource the information in places like Africa, we could get entirely updated figures. They are spending all this money to ascertain what diesel cost a year ago, when in the real world they need to know what it cost an hour ago. The younger generations virtually all have smartphones, which means you can talk to them direct to find out all you need to know about what is happening in the world and what the future holds. Knowledge no longer resides exclusively in universities and government departments, it is now available to everyone, and that is possibly going to be the major factor in helping those who feel they are trapped in the bottom five billion to improve their lives and lift themselves up to a level which gives them satisfaction.

- Whenever you have a good idea, ask yourself why it couldn't be made 10 times bigger, or even 100 times.
- Talk to everyone but think young. The young are the ones who know what the problems of the future are going to be. They will be the ones who find the answers.
- Whether you attend college or not, look for your education outside the existing system. Real life and the internet are the biggest school, and they are both working in real time.

21 | Future Generations

"Change is the law of life. And those who look only to the past or present are certain to miss the future."

—*John F. Kennedy*

"Education is the passport to the future, for tomorrow belongs to those who prepare for it today."

—*Malcolm X*

The widening of the gap between the two and a half billion haves and the five billion have-nots is very likely to speed up when the next generation reaches maturity, because the young people among the two and a half billion have grown up in a vastly different world to any generation before them. Their brains are wired differently. They are programmed to fit in to the world that is emerging from the technological advances of the last 20 years; they are fearless in the way they are pushing it forward. There has never been a generation like this before.

Those among them who are going to succeed will be able to think more clearly, more deeply, and faster than any generation in history, and they are ready and able to do that. They are going to be rethinking every model that the previous generations have ever taken for granted. Anyone who is not prepared for that is risking being trampled into extinction.

In his book, *Outliers*, Malcolm Gladwell points out the interesting fact that 14 of the 75 richest people in history are Americans who were born between 1832 and 1841. His conclusion is that in the 1860s and 1870s the American economy went through "perhaps the greatest transformation in its history." The railroads were being built and Wall Street emerged to rival London as a financial capital for the Industrial Revolution. "It was when all the rules by which the traditional economy functioned were broken and remade," Gladwell explains. "What that list says is that it really matters how old you were when that transformation happened."

The children of the technological revolution may well enjoy a similar level of success to that great entrepreneurial generation.

Many millennials have achieved unbelievable success in the last few years, but they were doing it on the backs of the generation that came before; the internet, GPS, fracking, microprocessors, and cell phones had all been invented before they grew up, but they learned quickly how to use them to improve their lives. They were born into the world before the major technological transformations had reached the general consumer, so they had to learn how the technologies worked just as their parents and grandparents did and benefited from them in much the same way. But the generation that is growing out of childhood now was born already knowing how people and technology worked together, so they were already fearless in the ways they used the advances the previous generations had put in place. They already know instinctively how to blow up models which have been the accepted way for doing things for centuries, and they are comfortable doing just that.

The millennials had a relatively easy ride in early adulthood, not only because they were able to take advantage of the technological advances made by the generation before them, but also because they were indulged by the baby-boomer parents who brought them up and allowed them to stay in school for five years longer, and to stay home for five years longer, getting into the full-time workforce five years later.

Although we baby boomers in the West were sent out to mow lawns and deliver papers as soon as we were physically able and were expected to contribute to our own financial situation, most of us did not insist that our children did the same. The Generation Z, however, which is coming of age at the time of this writing, has not been indulged to the same degree, and the differences in their levels of performance and achievement are going to be dramatic as a result.

The downside of that situation is that those who have not had the advantage of inheriting high intelligence or receiving a good education, and who are not networked in so that they can get jobs in the parts of the economy which are destined to grow exponentially, or to easily start businesses of their own, are not going to be able to keep up with the pace of change that this generation of high achievers is going to set.

There will not be many comfortable jobs for people who are just "good enough," people who in the past would have been taken on the payroll simply because their employers knew their parents or went to the same school. They are only going to be taken on if they are active contributors in the effort to make things better, because the more mundane jobs, which they would historically have been suited for, will now be automated. Those whose brains do not have really fast processing power, many of whom reside among the five billion, are not going to be able to keep up with the demands of the new world job market, and society will need to be restructured to ensure this doesn't result in a collapse of law and order. There will always be a certain number of blue-collar jobs, but it is bound to be a shrinking employment pool as robots become cheaper and more skilled. One of the side benefits of our crowdsourcing activities is that we will be offering employment opportunities to these people.

It is part of a continuum of change. People who once had to work down mines or as domestic servants, mercenary soldiers, or peasant farmers went into the factories during the Industrial Revolution and bettered their lives as a result, albeit only incrementally. As those jobs have gradually been taken over by machines and robots, a proportion of those workers have made their way into low-paid work (often on "zero hours contracts") in call centers and giant warehouses. But the modern corporate giants like Amazon and Alibaba do not need to hire as many people as were needed to build cars for Henry Ford or to bring enough coal up from underground to drive the trains and factories of the early twentieth century. And once drones and driverless cars become the norm, another level of employment opportunities will disappear. Who will need an Uber driver if a car can make the journey on its own? Who will need truck drivers or train drivers?

People who feel they have been left behind tend to believe they have nothing to lose by causing trouble and disruption to those who they see as having all the advantages they have been denied. The same people also have time on their hands and may well develop feelings of resentment toward those who appear to have everything that they do not, which will lead to flare-ups, demonstrations, and the sorts of revolutions that lead to violence, the destruction of property, and, in the most extreme cases, the overthrowing of governments.

It is indisputable that, at both pragmatic and ethical levels, something has to be done to help those who have been left behind financially to live happy, dignified, and rewarding lives. If, for instance, we can agree that a minimum wage is needed to achieve a dignified standard of living in the face of increased automation of jobs in Western countries, then the governments of those countries need to be prepared to make up the difference between whatever people are able to earn in menial jobs and whatever is agreed to be the minimum income level needed to live a decent life and to participate fully in society.

It is not practical to push the responsibility for caring for the five billion have-nots onto the business community alone because all they will do is increase automation or move their operations to places where the wages are lower, thereby increasing unemployment in their home countries and exacerbating the problem. If, however, a worker is able to make $400 per week in a menial job, but the agreed minimum for a dignified life is $600, then the government needs to design a system to pay the $200 difference.

That money will find its way back into the system almost immediately anyway. Those workers will not be able to store it away in bank accounts because they will need it to pay for groceries, rent, medication, or entertainment. By raising the living standards of the lowest-paid members of society, we would thereby be stimulating a variety of industries and trades, which would at the same time result in a raising of the living standards of everyone else above them.

There are any number of small ways in which the five billion can be successfully integrated with the two and a half billion. In the United States, for instance, we have special hospitals for veterans of the armed forces. We all, hopefully, agree that veterans should get the best possible healthcare at no charge, but on the whole the existing veterans' hospitals are terrible places and the waiting times for operations are appalling. It would be far more effective to blow up the whole model and simply give veterans cards which allow them to walk into any hospital or doctor's office knowing the bill for their treatment will be sent to the government. That way we would get rid of all the inefficient and expensive hospitals that have been set up separately for them and are not doing the job. By incorporating them into the mainstream we would also be restoring their dignity and closing the gap in the quality of the healthcare provided.

At another level, why do we still have roads with tollbooths which take cash and hold up the traffic? Why isn't every car simply fitted with an EZ-Pass, which gets sold on with the car to the next owner and that allows drivers to drive straight on without stopping? If we did that, we would cut down the lines, cut down pollution, increase productivity, and cut down the wage bills. All these problems, and a million more, are going to be solved by the next generation. President Obama broke a lot of models when he first stood for election. He was the first to extensively use social media, for instance, and micro-donations, but he was let down by his lack of experience and the fact that although he was a young president, he still belonged to a generation which was having to learn how to do these things rather than doing them instinctively. President Trump may be a much older man, but he has used social media in the same way as the younger generations, and soon Generation Z will be taking over the reins from the people currently working at the top when it comes to putting people in power.

Crowdsourcing and other social-media tools allow people to participate in communal events in completely new ways. Everyone wants to be part of a winning team, part of something bigger than themselves, something that will make a difference in the world, but not everyone wants to go out on the streets and physically campaign or protest.

Everyone wants to feel that there is meaning in their lives, so it shouldn't be hard to motivate millions of people to a common goal if you have the right tools. Castro did it before social media had even been dreamed of. Reagan and Thatcher both did it the old-fashioned way, despite being unpopular with large sections of the societies they were leading.

In the past, a great deal of power has been wielded by traditional print media, with their emphasis on personalities, scandals, and frequently negative attitudes to anything new or unusual. But these media owners are losing their power to a broader but consequently narrower-minded, audience. Young people are increasingly getting their news from social media, but if not carefully watched, their social-media profiles become echo chambers for their own views, being they are made up of like-minded people.

In the past, a major newspaper only had to expose one indiscretion on the part of a leader to bring them down, but now, if people believe in the ultimate cause, they will forgive a leader many of his or her flaws. We saw that most markedly with Trump, who the traditional media repeatedly tried to "shame" in the old-fashioned way and dramatically failed to do so. In the British general election of 2017 the tabloid media did everything they could to discredit the Labour leader, Jeremy Corbyn, and ensure an increased majority for Conservative Prime Minister Theresa May. When it came to Election Day, however, it was shown that young voters were not influenced by anything they had read in the papers and Mrs. May's majority was severely cut as a result.

Trump won, however, with an "anti-them" rather than a "pro-us" movement, which never lasts in my experience. It is always better to be "for" something positive rather than "against" something negative. (Another reason to stop calling charities "not for profit" organizations and to find something positive that they are "for.")

More and more career politicians are running for office with nothing of substance to say and no plan for how they will improve the lives of their followers, so they have to manufacture issues which they hope will stir the hearts of the electorate.

There is every reason to hope that, with their natural altruism and openness to positive change, the younger generation will improve things once they are in a position to do so.

Being against things rather than having a vision for how you are going to change them for the better is the political parallel of instigating incremental improvements in a dynamic business. It is lazy, uninspiring, and ultimately unproductive. The younger generations are fed up with hearing politicians arguing about everything and bad-mouthing one another rather than working together to fix things, and soon they will be the majority of the voting public.

- Be *for* something not *against* something.
- Those who are able to find a way to make the world more inclusive will be the biggest winners of the future. Imagine what you could achieve if you had a potential marketplace of seven and a half billion people.
- Imagine what could be achieved if we could harness the energies and abilities of everyone on the planet and direct them down a positive path.
- Think of new ways to improve the lives of the underserved — empowering and including them helps us all.

22 | The Power Shift

"When you get, give; when you learn, teach."

—*Maya Angelou*

There is a power shift in progress that goes way beyond the ubiquity of the internet and smartphones, and most people are underestimating the impact it is going to have on everything during the coming years. The shift is being caused by a combination of technology, social media, and the way people now absorb information, particularly the younger generations. It means that the top-down, centralized way we have been running the world for the last couple of centuries is no longer a viable model to follow.

Advances in technology, coupled with the end of the age of deference, have made it possible for us to create a real democracy where everyone truly has a chance at achieving the sort of lives they want to live. Within a few months of becoming president, Donald Trump was the most mocked figure in the world. People no longer automatically look to their leaders with respect. They no longer believe they can rely on those in power to look after their needs or take decisions on their behalf, as was shown by the British people voting for Brexit even though their leaders advised against it and by almost toppling an overconfident prime minister in the 2017 General Election. People all over the world are now truly close to "doin' it for themselves," as the Aretha Franklin lyric goes.

It is a time of enormous opportunity, but it is also possible that we will miss those opportunities due to the greed and conservatism of the various establishments which dominate the economy, both corporate and political – the people who in the past have held all the purse strings. As I've already said, there is also a danger that the wrong people will emerge to take advantage of these opportunities and that they will use them for destructive purposes.

ISIS showed how it is possible for a bunch of underdogs to create an illusion of themselves as a great and terrifying movement through the use of social media (the Wizard of Oz trick once again, only this time with demonstrations of real murder and cruelty involved). It just needs one deranged suicide bomber in a crowded place, one truck being driven into a crowd, or one brainwashed individual willing to carry out an execution on film and the entire connected world is left rightfully horrified and terrified.

These are some of the ways in which revolution can give a voice to those who wish others harm and who have agendas that push civilization backward rather than forward. But they are the minority and it is the majority that is winning the battle and will shift the power over all.

It is the individuals and companies with revolutionary ideas that will improve the lives of the majority who have the longest-lasting effects, as long as they are not stifled at birth. Uber is a good example of a company which had an idea huge numbers of people could see would be of benefit to them. When they met with opposition to their new model for transport, the company was able to harness the power of crowdsourcing and social media and use it to support their cause. There were people who wanted to stop them, like the traditional taxi services they threatened to replace. There were also those who disapproved of them, believing that they exploited and underpaid their workers or accused them of sexist practices, and if they are not able to fix those social issues, they will not succeed long term because young people are very attuned to company cultures. In the short term, however, the mass of the population wanted Uber's services and rejected the attempts by those who have dominated the cab industry up till now, and the authorities who they were lobbying, to deny them. There were also many people who found working for them a convenient way to earn a living.

Airbnb, YouTube, Alibaba, Wikipedia, and WikiLeaks have all, in their different ways, come about by popular demand, by the coming together of millions of individuals with overlapping needs and desires. All of these business initiatives were highly disruptive to the status quo and blew up parts of the old model; all of them are creative revolutions. The changes we are witnessing are largely possible because every individual can make their voice heard through Twitter, Instagram, YouTube, Facebook, or whatever other digital medium they use, and no one has to rely any more on a handful of newspapers or television stations to receive their news or to disseminate their messages. When the young people rose up in the late sixties to campaign for peace, to protest about the war in Vietnam, and to fight for the civil rights of the black population, they started a movement that has continued to roll ever since. But it only rolled slowly. The improvements were only incremental. Before them the suffragettes fought for women's rights – sometimes even giving their lives to the cause. Some of the wrongs and inequalities they were campaigning against 100 years ago, however, are still with us. Women, for instance, are still paid less than their male counterparts in the West, and in many parts of the world they are still treated as the possessions of their fathers and husbands. Imagine how much faster the suffragettes would have been able to progress had they had even half the global social-media power of modern movements and revolutions.

Information is now disseminated by millions of individuals rather than a handful of "opinion formers," as they were once known, and absorbed on the same individual level. Just as billions of raindrops will eventually create an ocean, so billions of voices all speaking together can create a movement in a space where nothing existed before. Democracy now has the tools it needs to fulfill its potential and work for everyone.

There is a fundamental change happening in the ways power can be gained, wielded, shifted, and manipulated. It is potentially migrating from the old holders of power to new people who understand how to exploit the technology that allows more people to have a voice and for more voices to be heard and to communicate with one another.

President Trump drew attention to this underlying power shift with his constant cries of "fake news" whenever the newspapers printed anything that he disagreed with, but the change was already underway before that and was partly responsible for bringing him to power in the first place by giving his campaign far more coverage than it deserved at any intellectual level. Who, a year before it happened, could ever have imagined a day when Donald Trump would get into the oval office? (Apart from the creators of *The Simpsons*, of course, who predicted it 16 years before it happened in order to create a laughable satire to illustrate that all Americans had gone insane.)

With each new generation these skills are going to become more and more refined. Imagine how well people like Mark Zuckerberg of Facebook understand the algorithms that govern how we communicate with one another. If someone who wants to win an election can communicate on a one-to-one basis with every potential voter, the chances are they are going to succeed in becoming a leader, should that be their objective.

It sounds like a positive, democratic shift, and in some ways it is. But the owners of the individual voices which come together to bring someone new to power will not automatically be the ones who benefit from the changes the new leadership brings about. Their voices will inevitably be harvested and turned into votes by the political classes and into profits by the business classes, just as their physical labor and their money have been in the past, unless we make a conscious effort to avoid that happening. If we believe that the amount of power once wielded by the owners of the traditional media such as newspapers and broadcast television was dangerous, then we should be aware that the power that could potentially fall into the hands of the technologically savvy new generation is infinitely greater. It is possible that we will one day look back on the times when media owners like Rupert Murdoch built their empires and they will seem like no more than local barons compared to the global elites who have replaced them.

If, however, the divide continues to widen between the haves and the have-nots, crowdsourcing could develop into the weapon that the have-nots can utilize to ensure they do not become entirely crushed, and we need to ensure that it will be more effective and more positive than the older models of protest and revolution, where people took to the streets with bricks and suicide bombs, and which nearly always ended up being brutally crushed and eradicated by the incumbent powers.

All past changes in the power structure began from grass-roots movements. They were then nourished by the disenchantment of the have-nots, whether they were women or blacks or young people, who suddenly found themselves able to communicate in order to organize effectively and put a structure in place to express how disaffected they were with the status quo. Like the traditionally powerful people before them, the newly powerful can also create the illusion of having discovered a solution to everyone's problems, even if none actually exists.

In the developing world there is the equivalent of seven New York City populations moving to or being born in urban environments each year.

> According to the Woodrow Wilson Center, a youth "explosion" is also underway. According to their study, by 2030, 60 percent of the world's population will live in cities and 60 percent oi those residents will be under the age of 18. That is a staggering potential shift in power.

What are those young people living in the world's cities, the vast majority of whom possess scant financial resources, going to do to communicate, entertain, and barter with one another? At the moment it is impossible to predict, but it will certainly be a very different model to anything that has come before. They are already modifying and jerry-rigging technology in any new way they can, but inventions like YouTube, Facebook, and iTunes may soon look as old-fashioned as vinyl records and *The Ed Sullivan Show*.

In many cases, particularly in Africa, these new cities, blossoming out of poverty, filled with people driven from the countryside by necessity and by the temptations of the modern material world, do not have sufficient effective infrastructure for the levels of growth they are undergoing. They do not have the schools, the hospitals, the roads, or the houses that are needed for their existing populations, never mind the floods of migrants arriving each year from the villages, smallholdings, and rice fields. That lack of infrastructure dramatically increases the numbers of have-nots at the very poorest end of the scale, the people who are entirely unable to get a foot on the ladder when it comes to building good lives for themselves and for their families. If you have no house and no job and there is no welfare system in place, what options are left to you? Only begging or crime or moving on to a new place where you will undoubtedly be unwelcome because you will be seen as a threat to the pleasant living standards of those who are already there.

If a poor family is living in the countryside, like my family was when they lived in Galway, Ireland, it is possible for them to fend for themselves with a few chickens and a few vegetables, even if they are uneducated. In these vast new cities, that is no longer possible. If you are not educated and machines can do all the jobs you are qualified for, then your only hope is that society will support you, unless we rethink the model.

These dispossessed people may have voices and political power through the advances in technology which have reached them, such as the smartphones in their pockets, but they don't yet have money, they don't have ownership of any place that they can call a home, they don't have the capital to start businesses and they don't have the space to live comfortable or even settled lives. Yet day in and day out they are forced to watch those who do, those who have been more fortunate than them in the families that they were born into, growing more and more prosperous and comfortable within economic frameworks that favor the few.

If the power shifts toward these huge and growing numbers of angry, poor, uneducated people, and they decide to use it, then the potential for major disruption is virtually endless.

One way or another, the young people will take matters into their own hands and will build alternative economies. We've already seen this in Africa, where, over the past several years, the smartphone has almost entirely circumvented the traditional bank as the preferred mode of payment and cash transfer. For users it has been one of the most liberating developments of the past few decades and the implications for traditional financial services institutions have been tremendous; yet no government anticipated it and not many of the big banks either. In the West we have seen it in the rise of "free" entertainment and services online. Where once there were pay walls surrounding every form of entertainment, it is now possible for people to watch movies and communicate with one another virtually free of charge twenty-four hours a day if they have a computer or a smartphone and an internet connection.

At the same time, wages at the bottom of the market have shrunk and the cost of fulfilling basic needs like food and housing have soared, making many of the younger generation feel excluded from the mainstream.

The days in which technology was "introduced" by authorities, carefully doled out and centrally controlled, are long gone. Technology in the hands of the youth of the developing world provides the easiest form of revolution – and will give them a chance at gaining many sorts of freedom.

What this will mean for other corporations with deep roots in the developing world is becoming clear; they are equally vulnerable to power shifts away from central control to a far more decentralized, populist model. If banks were the low-hanging fruit, we now have to start thinking about how developments in communications might shift power away from other sectors such as television stations, shopping centers, sports networks, security services, and transportation.

There's obviously a moral problem with leaving this many people behind, and there is also a physical problem if the new technology empowers them to disrupt society. The shift in power isn't necessarily going to solve the problem of the gap between the haves and the have-nots, but it makes it potentially more volatile and more dangerous, as demonstrated by the rise of ISIS, the genocides and uprisings going on all over Africa, and the potential for cyber attacks from rogue states and rogue individuals which could close down whole sections of society in seconds.

Many of the worst crimes, like the genocides, are awarded less time, space, and visibility in the media of the developed world because the countries involved have no oil and therefore no voice at the international table (and because the international news crews don't want to spend too much time there). One terrorist attack at an iconic site in London or Paris will fill the news media for weeks, yet every day in the developing world far greater atrocities are happening and going relatively unreported. That situation will inevitably change if the gap between the haves and have-nots continues to widen and the atrocities threaten to spread further into the developed world.

Lack of broadband and wireless network access in many developing countries remains a stumbling block to their progress. No community that is cut off from broadband can hope to compete with one that is fully connected any more than countries without roads or railroad networks could.

Even in rural areas of the United States and Western Europe, inadequate broadband access seems to be a problem that should have been solved long ago. Around the world, there are an estimated four billion people who don't yet have adequate broadband speeds, most of them with no internet access at all (interesting, and significant in that rounded-off figure is not far off the estimated number of have-nots). Getting the internet to them should be as great a priority as getting fresh water or medical supplies to them, and it should be a great deal simpler to achieve because it does not involve building power stations or laying pipelines across deserts. Once it has been achieved, then other developments, like the reliable provision of water and power, also become easier to organize.

Until recently, the power to provide internet access resided with the handful of incumbent communications providers, who usually had a lock on cable, phone, and wireless services. That situation is now unsustainable. Ireland is now the world leader in using government money and influence to rollout broadband to every single home.

In Cairo, as another example, there are reported to be four times as many smartphones as there are data plans. That means that millions of people are using creative solutions to access the internet with their smartphone. Operating "off the grid" and away from the prying eyes of "Big Brother" is going to be increasingly the norm in the next wave of technology. What these enterprising young people do is take their smartphones to a McDonald's, or another place with Wi-Fi, to download the content they want.

We are also seeing the rise of inexpensive, mobile and portable networks that effectively establish an "internet-in-a-box" alternative. With this technology, creating remote hubs can provide access without the huge infrastructure start-up costs that have proved to be stumbling blocks to progress in the past.

What will the young citizens in bustling developing world cities do online once they have unlimited access? Some will undoubtedly be drawn to the networks of terror, and the majority must be constantly vigilant and willing to fight that. But most will see access to the online world as a lifeline – a new source of power and creativity, a way to improve their own lives and a way to improve the world we all live in. It will give them a voice, through crowdsourcing developments, where before they were entirely invisible and their voices unheard.

When it comes to fighting against those who would terrorize others, we need to rethink that model too, because whatever we have been doing for the past few decades has not worked. If sending over drones and bombs was an effective way of defeating the enemy, we would not still be embroiled in the longest-running war of modern civilization. The Western method of making war failed in Vietnam and it has failed in the Middle East, but still we keep on doing the same things, wasting money and energy, destroying lives, destroying infrastructure, and breeding yet more enmity and hatred for the future.

So yes, the internet and technology feed the possibility for continuous revolution, but this revolution involves more than just a change in the tools we use. It represents a shift in influence toward those who previously were unbanked, unaffiliated, and unconnected. We should be doing everything we can to spread any technology that offers a better way for future generations to channel their impulse for mischief and disruption, while guarding against those who believe that process should involve violence for the purposes of spreading either oppression or terror.

Since the advent of telecoms competition thirty years ago – when the first incumbent telcos didn't recognize that copper was dead and fiber was the future – corporate and governmental behemoths have had a strange blind spot about disruption, either ignoring it or discounting it until it's on top of them, at which point they find themselves battling for their very existence. It is always a lot smarter to look for disruption when it is approaching and run to meet it while it's still a dot on the horizon than to wait until it has run you over.

Technology-fueled disruption is everywhere, and, like the social-media-driven US election, it should be sending off warning flares to big business, because it's demonstrating how starkly the center of gravity is moving to the masses. What happened to the elite of Washington and London in 2016 will be happening to them too, if it isn't already.

Across all sectors, there exist industries so accustomed to being in control of their marketplaces that they forget what it's like not to be in the driver's seat: entertainment, broadcasting, and transportation being obvious examples. Organizations in these powerful sectors have no memory of how it feels not to have their hands firmly on the levers that move the world. They will consequently be hard pushed to come up with any responses that might save them when they wake up to find that everything has changed and they don't automatically own the world any more.

Archimedes said: "Give me a place to stand and with a lever I will move the earth." Consider for a moment what those traditional levers of power were: control of the means of production, distribution, publication, and transportation. Controlling these gave an organization not just power, but also the undisputed ability to command public attention. But while the traditional emphasis was on what the controlling entity could do, power today is more about who has the most influence.

Brexit in Britain and the Trump and Macron victories in the United States and France aren't the first demonstrations of this shift in power. The late Shimon Peres commented that he wielded more power after being president and prime minister of Israel than during his time in office. "Power today is about influence," he said. "It's not about what you can do, it's about what you can get others to do." Though Peres no longer controlled the apparatus of government, he was still well connected and used only his powers of persuasion to ask others to volunteer to help him.

An influencer who can convince millions of people to take action can shape policy, alter a country's political future, and agitate for change against the will of incumbent government officials. Witness the ongoing lobbying power of companies like Airbnb, which continues to leverage its mass user base to pressure city officials who want to impose caps on the number of rental days that can be made available on the platform.

This kind of influence is global, massively distributed, and rapidly deployable; a potentially frightening prospect for the traditional ruling elites, especially because influence itself can be an illusion.

In the social-media age, "influencers" may in fact be nobodies who've cultivated an alluring message and a strong grasp of how the technological indicators of influence can be faked – just like the Wizard of Oz. A trending hashtag on Twitter or a million-subscriber YouTube following might be no more than massively coordinated social-media bubbles, but that will not be how they appear to the uninitiated. And what of companies who attempt to co-opt (or perhaps "corrupt" would be a more apt word) the new influencers of the social-media age for the purposes of sponsorship and promotion? Social-media celebrity endorsements are a questionable effort by industry to buy and harness influence that they have not strictly earned. The number of YouTube stars with book deals and brand sponsorships continues to grow and says a lot about big business's realization that influence is everything.

But what if those celebs' influence is revealed to be an illusion? Or the people themselves turn out to be something very different from how they seemed? (The dramatic and well-publicized fall from grace of former heroes such as O.J. Simpson and Lance Armstrong bears witness to how badly things can go wrong when widespread public illusions are shattered.)

The idea within big business that influence can be monetized is still prevalent and is entirely understandable as a theory. The execution, however, can never be entirely risk-managed. By buying influence in this top-down way, the old companies with old power structures are seeking to use influence to leverage the crowd rather than to empower it.

A seminal article on this idea of the power shift in the *Harvard Business Review* closed by saying this about empowerment:

> Those capable of channeling the power of the crowd must turn their energies to. . .redesigning society's systems and structures to meaningfully include and empower more people. The greatest test for the conductors of new power will be their willingness to engage with the challenges of the least powerful. (https://hbr.org/2014/12/understanding-new-power.)

I believe it is incumbent on individual corporations and governments to seek out ways to deliver that empowerment, and they should not consider them to be acts of charity. Findyr, Alchemy, Emergent Data Group, ALTV, and all of Granahan McCourt's social-media and crowdsourcing investments are highly commercial ventures, but all are aimed at creating value for the crowd as well as for the brands who want to leverage the power of that crowd.

Maybe that is what business is going to look like in the age of influence: new, win–win paradigms that recognize the emergence of populist power and that find ways to deliver benefit and reward to the crowd in return for their collective action.

The organizations and entrepreneurs who can adjust to these shifts in power, who can rebalance and find their sea legs while also managing risk, are the ones who will weather this change. Those who underestimate the storminess of the waters that now surround us may not be so lucky.

Dictators who are fearful of this shift in power all too often resort to brute force and suppression of the technology in the hope of maintaining the status quo, but their success can only ever be short term because the change is real and inevitable. Unless, of course, we decide to destroy all the scientific advances of the last few centuries and take ourselves back to the Dark Ages, which is what some dictators such as Pol Pot in Cambodia have tried before, and some fanatics, like the leaders of the Taliban and ISIS, would like to achieve again.

> Understanding past trends no longer means you can predict the future, as both journalists and pollsters have discovered when their predictions have been proved to be wildly wide of the mark by election results. On top of all this uncertainty is the "fake news" and the bad facts disguised as real facts. Political and business bets have become harder and harder to get right because the information you make them on is becoming less and less trustworthy.

So we are moving from incremental change to blowing up the model, and there are a number of factors driving that. First there was globalization, the speed of which was probably accelerated by the fall of communism and the victory of capitalism and the arrival of the internet. There has been more exposure of the haves to the have-nots through social media, and there has been a growing ability to form groups or coalitions because of social media. Putting all these factors together has led to faster change and greater uncertainty, which is proving to be a challenge to the politicians as well as the business people.

- Recognize that there are enormous power shifts underway and look for opportunities within the new structure.
- There is no point trying to cling to traditional ways of doing things once the new ways have proved to be more popular and to benefit greater numbers of people.

23

The Power of Immigration

"If you go back to 1800 everybody was poor. I mean everybody. The Industrial Revolution kicked in, and a lot of countries benefited, but by no means everyone."

—*Bill Gates*

In 2016 the total of displaced people was 65 million, mostly by war but also by national disasters and economic circumstances. That's around two people for every second of the year. It is possibly the biggest issue and potential threat to world peace and to continued prosperity, but not because of the immigrants themselves.

The rise of nationalism in the West has been partly fueled by a short-term fear of the numbers of immigrants arriving in search of work or shelter, but as I mentioned earlier, in the long term these people are the most motivated workers in the world and the most likely to create beneficial changes wherever they settle. They are our greatest hope for creating a revolution that will ensure a prosperous future for all. They are the ones most likely to be able to narrow the gap between the haves and the have-nots, through creative entrepreneurship and relentless execution.

These are the people who are willing to smuggle themselves across the Mexican border into America in the dead of night, or cross an ocean in an overcrowded dinghy which is extremely likely to sink, in order to start a new life in a European country that is apparently hostile to their arrival, where they don't speak the language or have any family network to fall back on for support. They are the sorts of people who have already proved that they are brave enough to blow up the model of their lives and start again. In many cases they have given up their homes and possessions, their professions, and possibly their families too, with the overriding purpose of trying to build a better life. Many have been willing to risk investing large amounts of money, often the last money that they possess, in fees to potentially criminal organizations and individuals, who promise to smuggle them to destinations they know virtually nothing about. These people have already shown enormous courage and determination in circumstances that are almost unimaginable to those of us fortunate enough never to have experienced them.

People who are willing to work 12 hours a day picking tomatoes in the blazing sun for slave wages in order to send money back to support their families, while they themselves live in appalling conditions, are exactly the sort of people you want to have living next door to you and working alongside you. They, rather than the people who live comfortable lives on the capital and infrastructures built up by previous generations, are the ones who have the courage, the strength, the motivation, and the vision needed to blow up the model and create a new and better society.

These are the most truly entrepreneurial people in the world. Their approach to risk is entirely different to anyone who lives securely and safely in the country of their own birth (and probably the birth of their parents and grandparents). As a result, they are often enormously successful in any venture they undertake.

Those who live safely and comfortably in the lands of their ancestors, however, do not always welcome the arrival of these people, who they fear will change things and disrupt their way of life, taking their jobs, driving down wages and overloading the infrastructure of the host country. If your life is comfortable already, you are not likely to want anything to change in the short term, however creative the process might be in the long term. By trying to stem the movement of migrants, however, these reactionaries are behaving exactly like the soon-to-be-extinct organizations and the insecure dictators who attempt to hold back the tidal forces of inevitable change. They are condemning themselves to grow stale and slow and to being left behind by the more enterprising cultures and greater ambitions of the people emerging from the developing world.

The aging populations of countries in the West are an enormous opportunity for the younger populations in the emerging countries, and many of them are taking advantage of their positions at the bottom of the pile, where they have everything to gain and virtually nothing to lose. Just as the executives sitting at the top of large corporations are more resistant to taking risks by making revolutionary changes than young entrepreneurs, the citizens of countries where the average incomes and standards of living are low have less to lose, have been through greater hardships and are therefore more likely to make creative and revolutionary choices. The best and brightest of their people are more motivated to be creative and to work hard to execute their plans because they want to get themselves and their families out of the environments they are in and they have to strive hard in whatever environment they move to unless they want to live in extreme poverty.

These are all the ingredients that you would have seen in America at the beginning of the twentieth century, during the time when the United States' greatest entrepreneurial thinkers and doers were thriving, and in Britain at the end of the previous century, when they had an expanding empire and were creating the giant physical industries that would dominate the world for the next century and eventually lift the living standards of virtually every single person on the planet. Even the poorest people on earth have gained at least some benefit, either directly or indirectly, from inventions such as the railroads, the internal combustion engine, and electricity. There is a perception that America might not still be full of great entrepreneurs, as it was 100 years ago. In reality, many of the biggest corporations are merely taking advantage of the achievements of previous generations, such as the family descendants of the great wealth creators of history. There are far more opportunities for business people to rethink the model and make improvements to many millions of lives in the developing economies than in the mature ones, and far more individuals who are willing to take the big risks that are necessary if you wish to make big gains.

Where the American system is uniquely helpful to potential creative revolutionaries is in the way that failure is not considered a stigma, and people are encouraged to pick themselves up after failing and to try again, not just in business, but politically, reputationally, ethically, morally, and every other way. Our bankruptcy system and the many ways in which we can gain access to venture capital and debt all benefit those who want to be creative entrepreneurs. The infrastructure is there if people are only willing to take the risks and do the work which is required. In many cases, however, those opportunities are not spotted or exploited.

Most people would prefer to take a job they consider to be secure, in an industry which has already proven itself to be a success, but that security is an illusion. These jobs are no longer secure, as they might have been fifty years ago, because these mature companies often only increase their earnings in a competitive global economy by laying people off and looking for ways to cut costs. It is the entrepreneurial start-ups which actually provide the potential for security, because they are set on growth paths, hiring more and more people as they expand, just as the railroad barons and Henry Ford were doing 100 years ago, and Walmart, IBM, and McDonald's were doing 60 years ago.

> It is the law of the jungle that once an animal becomes old and slow, as all corporations and all countries eventually do, it will be replaced as the leader of the pack by a leaner, hungrier animal.

Businesses and governments who do not disrupt the model and start again, as these brave immigrants have done with their lives, are inevitably going to be destroyed by disintermediation, by crowdsourcing, and by the unstoppable forward movement of globalism. My brother Frank and I have recently been thinking about ways that we could work together more, combining our very different business approaches to greatest effect. We worked together a lot at the start of our careers and would like to do so again now that we are getting closer to the end (although both of us claim vehemently that we feel like we are only just getting started). One of the areas that we are both passionate about is finding ways to help young people, and people who are arriving in countries as immigrants for one reason or another, to be able to succeed and to change things that need changing. In this time of shifting power, Frank can see the benefits of my bottom-upward approach to problem solving, while I can appreciate the value of his top-down approach as a way to scale my own business ambitions.

- High levels of immigration inevitably lead to greater prosperity in the future.
- Only by welcoming those who have not yet been fortunate, and by helping them to prosper, can we hope to close the gap between the haves and the have-nots.
- People who have had to struggle are nearly always going to be more motivated to be creative and to work harder, so don't let bumps in the road get you down.

24

The Sheer Joy of Being a Creative Revolutionary

"Art, freedom, and creativity will change society faster than politics."
—*Victor Pinchuk*

So, if truly creative entrepreneurs are born rather than made, as I think is usually the case, can they ever stop being creative and settle for the status quo?

There have been a few times in my career when I have been asked if I would be interested in taking a salaried job running a major company, or becoming a political appointee, or running for office. The offers have been tempting and, as I have already admitted, I never like saying "no" to any opportunity for a new experience. I have given each invitation a lot of thought before answering, fearful that either way I might end up regretting my decision if I acted too hastily.

Being on a guaranteed salary and bonus package would certainly be a much easier way to make money because, unlike entrepreneurs, senior executives don't have to start anything themselves and they don't have to risk any of their own money in the process. For those very reasons, however, I am not convinced that they always deserve the high monetary rewards that they manage to negotiate for themselves. Consequently, I can't help feeling that it would be unsatisfying to know that the money was going to go into my bank account at the end of each month regardless of whether or not I had achieved good results. Would it not be hard to remain fully committed and motivated under such conditions?

I also know myself well enough to know that I would never want to be limited to doing just one job, however arduous or responsible or high status it might be. Sometimes chasing so many different strands at the same time can be a problem for me, because I am not always able to give each one the attention that it needs, but it is the stimulation of being able to follow up on every idea and opportunity that comes to me, being able to chase every dream, that makes being a creative entrepreneur so exciting. That is why I always said "no" to the job offers.

On one occasion, someone else, who knew me well, actually said "no" on my behalf. I was being offered the job to be the CEO of a Fortune 100 company by a headhunter over lunch in a small private company dining room high up on the thirty-seventh floor of the J.P. Morgan building.

Jimmy Lee, the famed J.P. Morgan dealmaker and vice-chairman, was hosting the lunch. A few months earlier, he had been to my house in Ireland and had seen what I was doing there by way of restoration of the buildings and planting out of the gardens. The headhunter was pitching for me to take the job. Both myself and the company in question were big clients of J.P. Morgan. It was an attractive offer, but just as I opened my mouth to speak Jimmy Lee interrupted.

"That's not for Dave," he said. "What he does is create stuff where there was nothing before. He's bought this piece of land in Ireland, with buildings that look like Ground Zero, but he's transforming it, turning a piggery into a guesthouse and a chicken coop into a bathroom. He's built his own private pub from one of the stables and the cowshed is now this amazing walled garden. He took something that looked like a piece of shit and turned it into something beautiful."

I am very proud of the home I have created in Ireland. It is an old farmhouse built among the ruins of a castle. I bought it sight unseen because I reckoned that a castle takes about five generations to build and if the situation isn't perfect then the inhabitants just move on, so the chances were that this was going to be a good piece of land. I was pretty sure it would be dry, and it would have a good view, because inhabitants of castles needed to be able to see potential attackers coming from a distance. It would have a source of fresh water, and

I could see from the map it was on a lake. My theory was that if the house was terrible, I could always pull it down as long as the land was good.

I called friends of mine who knew the area, one of whom was a publican, another a builder, and another a lawyer, and they all agreed that it was a great piece of land, so I bid for it and got it.

I came to look at it with a builder. There was a tree growing through the roof and he was listing all the things we would have to do to it, ". . .and we'll have to put some heat into the house."

"There's no heat in the house?" I asked. "So, how do they get hot water?"

He turned and looked at me with raised eyebrows. "Water?"

There was no water, no power, no anything in the house. It was basically as it had been when it was built several hundred years before. A little later I was in the area with my daughter, Alex, who was by then 10 years old. We were on our way to dinner somewhere and she was all dressed up. I wanted to show her the house from the original castle driveway, but the cobbles had long ago sunk beneath a sea of damp peat and water. More or less from the moment they could walk, I alternated taking the children on business trips with me. In both cases I believe it developed their love of business and hard work and they both picked up a lot, albeit in very different ways. These days I take great pleasure in watching them interacting on these trips, no longer just observing, and even if they eventually decide that the business world is not for them long term, I believe they have learned how to approach problems in a revolutionary way in order to make a difference in whatever world they choose to enter.

"Dad," Alex said solemnly as she sank up to her ankles in mud, "I only have two pairs of good shoes and I really don't like the other pair, so technically I only have one good pair of shoes and they are getting ruined."

I assured her that it would be worth it once she saw the house and the view, but the sight of the ivy-covered ruin did little to raise her spirits. I brought my lawyer up the same path a few days later and proudly gestured to the house.

"Looks like fucking 9/11 to me," he grumbled.

Back in the dining room at J.P. Morgan, the headhunter asked: "What's your point, Jimmy?"

"Dave likes to create stuff from nothing. Taking a job at a company that has already been created will never happen."

Once the headhunter had left, I said, "I think you're right, Jimmy, but I probably could have made a lot of money doing that job."

"Dave, what you do is start with an idea and you create something. You should stick with what you are really good at and not try to do something else."

I think he was right, and I hear similar comments from my brother Frank and my mentor Walter Scott. It could be compared to the difference between buying a beautiful painting and creating a painting of your own. Your painting may not be quite as beautiful as the one you could have bought, but it will be all yours and that is the most satisfying feeling in the world. It's the same feeling as creating a new company rather than being hired as a caretaker for one that is already big and successful. I hope my two kids stay in business with me, and if they do, I'm sure they will create something new, different, and better than what they started with.

Jimmy died unexpectedly a few years ago and I miss him greatly. We always used to call one another whenever either of us needed cheering up.

If you are CEO of a giant company you also run the risk of losing touch with what is going on underneath you, ending up carrying the can for something you didn't do personally. As an example, Bernie Ebbers, a guy I knew pretty well, who was CEO of WorldCom, the big telecoms company I had previously been on the board of after we sold MFS to them for $14.6 billion, ended up being jailed for life. During the trial, the judge said that if Bernie didn't know about the inappropriate accounting practices going on in the company, as CEO he should have. If he didn't know what was going on, I'm sure he regrets losing touch with what was going on below him.

During the dot-com boom and bust, a lot of people lost huge amounts of money and many of the CEOs of those companies made themselves a great deal of money by selling their stock when it was up high, which made a lot of people angry. Working as I do as an entrepreneur, I am always using my own money alongside other people's, which means if other people lose I lose too, and vice versa. I never get out of a venture until everyone else is out either. Other investors can therefore feel confident that I am going to be doing all I can to make sure none of us loses money, and that if disaster does strike, it will affect me as much as them.

After the dot-com bust the authorities then went into these companies to investigate what had happened and when they did they found that a lot of bad things had been going on (Enron was the most famous example of a company that was using crooked accounting practices during that period). WorldCom stock had tanked, everyone had lost a great deal of money, and they found out that among other things, the CFO had basically been amortizing the cost of fiber over a long period in cases where the appropriate accounting method was to expense in one year, thereby making the earnings look better than they were. A lot of companies years ago did that sort of thing and some got no more than a slap on the wrists although it was going against generally accepted accounting principles. Eventually, however, the authorities were accusing WorldCom of $11 billion of misstatements and wanted to make an example of them. During my time on the board I had been part of the audit committee and yet during the investigations no one from the government ever asked me if I knew anything about accounting fraud. If they had I would have been able to tell them that nothing was visible to us, and so it was perfectly feasible that it would not have been visible to Bernie either.

The authorities threatened to put the CFO in jail for accounting fraud, and also for tax fraud because if the numbers were wrong it would mean the company had paid the wrong amount of tax. And because they sent the tax form through the mail it became a mail fraud too, and because they wired money it was also a wire fraud. They were building the charges to make them look really bad and then they asked if Bernie Ebbers had known what was going on. Scott Sullivan, the CFO said "no" and they could find no evidence that he was lying. He said it a few times and then suggested that he might get a lighter sentence if the authorities were able to pin something on a really big fish, so he changed his answer to "yes." As a result, Bernie was put in prison for life, being given more time than a guy who tried to blow up Los Angeles International Airport, which doesn't seem right. I personally don't think he was guilty of as many crimes as he was accused, particularly as he was buying millions of dollars' worth of WorldCom stock with his own money right up to the end, which doesn't seem like the behavior of someone who knew there was an accounting fraud, and nor does anyone else I speak to who knows anything about the case. But that kind of thing can happen to you if you lose connection with what is happening below. Bernie is a good man and he was the victim of a politically motivated witch hunt. I wrote to him in jail recently, and he wrote back a very touching letter talking about how it was not only a waste of his life to have locked him away like that, but it was a waste of a lot of other people's lives too. It wasn't like he was a danger to society, so it would have been much better to punish him by setting him to work teaching in schools or cleaning highways for the minimum wage. Any money he might be able to make above that could have gone into a fund to help pay off shareholders who had lost money on WorldCom. There must be a thousand more creative ways of dealing with the situation than locking him in a cell and throwing away the key.

The US Judicial System, which has been growing and developing incrementally for several centuries, is way overdue for being blown up and started again. The fact that we have the largest prison population in the world (substantially more than two million people and the second highest per capita after the Seychelles), plus the fact that approximately 12 percent of the American population is African-American but in 2014 they made up 35 percent of jail inmates, suggest that it is time to rethink the model.

Kids signing up for university courses may believe they want to become entrepreneurs in order to get rich, but it has never been the money that has led me to follow this path. If I had wanted money I would have aimed to climb the corporate ladder in one of the big blue-chip companies. Instead I have risked losing everything that I have made at least 10 times over in my life, and sometimes I have lost most of it for the sheer exhilaration of creating something from nothing.

I became an entrepreneur for the joy of doing things differently. It is the excitement of being able to rethink the model and change how things are done in the world, in ways that eventually bring benefits to everyone, which makes it such a very great adventure. I was quoted by the BBC as saying: "I love business and I love doing battle. I love competition and I love to win. I like to accomplish stuff and I like to build stuff. . . I like all those better than golf, or drinking, or watching TV."

- Don't set out with the aim of making money.
- Know that you can't do anything really interesting without the support of others.
- Set out to be revolutionary and creative and then, if you are good at what you do and able to execute your plans, you might just become rich as a result.
- By the time that happens, however, you won't care because you will be having too much fun.

Epilogue

"May your hands always be busy/May your feet always be swift/May you have a strong foundation/When the winds of changes shift/May your heart always be joyful May your song always be sung/And may you stay forever young."

—*Bob Dylan*

As my mentor and friend Walter Scott tells me, ignore fads and focus on trends. So here are some trends that we should all focus on as we strive to lead a more entrepreneurial life and navigate through the disruptive and revolutionary change that's inevitable.

The world will continue to become more open, transparent, and globally connected, regardless of any campaigns by the nationalist leaders of countries who might want to close borders, build walls, and erect trade barriers.

The vast majority of the world's population wants to be connected; people want to communicate with one another.

That movement is unstoppable, so despite short-term political setbacks, the peaceful global revolution will continue in the long term, with improved telecommunications services at its heart.

There will continue to be expansion of wireless solutions which will allow handsets to be further from fiber and still receive world-class connectivity.

There will be an increase in wholesale, open access networks, sometimes supported by government money. In the past, the big cable and phone companies have wanted to own and control their own networks, but now there are so many providers in the market that users are starting to move off-network into open access platforms, viewing connectivity as a utility. This trend will become more established globally.

Personal data will continue to become increasingly portable, providing greater access to information for every individual and for services such as investment, healthcare, entertainment, and education. This will be the first step in bringing more control and order to the wilder frontiers of the internet. Regulation will be needed for personal data portability, although like most regulation, it will come later than it should and be more complicated than it needs to be. The more hopeful ideals behind the founding of the internet were to create equality, transparency, and access to information for the masses. Although a lot of those ideals have come to pass, there has also been an inevitable downside, leading to the creation and dissemination of vast amounts of deception and disinformation, leading to some very bad, "populist" decisions being taken by both governments and corporations. Careful regulation will undoubtedly help here, but a personal commitment to stepping outside of your own social echo-chamber is a healthy first start.

The trend for the crowdsourcing of video content will continue to grow, making every corner of the world more visible and more comprehensible to others, continuing to erode the power of the mainstream media, Hollywood, and other supposed traditional gatekeepers of culture.

Global society is becoming more open all the time, and the effects are snowballing. Those who are trying to stop it are swimming against the tide of popular culture and creating an atmosphere of mistrust and anxiety which could lead to civil unrest, but in spite of all that, I don't believe that the revolution can be stopped now.

These developments will eventually affect every single person on the planet, not just the political or business establishments. We will soon all be connected, from the richest to the poorest, with all the opportunities that affords for creating better lives for everyone. If, however, we do not all think and act creatively we could end up destroying everything we have achieved so far and sabotaging everything that could be achieved in the future.

"No matter what happens in your life remember someone has it worse. Try, as hard as it seems, to always accept what has happened. Put one foot in front of the other and move forward, always forward."

—*Katherine McCourt, author's mother*

About the Author

David McCourt is one of the world's most successful, award-winning business people, widely recognized for using technology and innovation to improve the lives of underserved communities by deploying new revolutionary ways of thinking.

Over the last 30 years he has founded or bought 20 companies in 9 countries, becoming a leader in the technology, media, and telecommunications industries.

McCourt is also an Emmy Award–winning producer, and his work has included prime-time documentaries that highlight the world's most prominent problems, starring some of the world's most famous actors including Michael Douglas, Angelina Jolie, and Meg Ryan. McCourt's production of the critically acclaimed children's TV series *Reading Rainbow* became the most-watched show in the classroom in the United States.

McCourt is currently Founder and Chairman of the worldwide investment firm Granahan McCourt Capital.